Cambridge Elements

Elements in the Philosophy of Immanuel Kant
edited by
Desmond Hogan
Princeton University
Howard Williams
University of Cardiff
Allen Wood
Indiana University

KANT'S NATURAL PHILOSOPHY

Marius Stan
Boston College

Shaftesbury Road, Cambridge CB2 8EA, United Kingdom

One Liberty Plaza, 20th Floor, New York, NY 10006, USA

477 Williamstown Road, Port Melbourne, VIC 3207, Australia

314–321, 3rd Floor, Plot 3, Splendor Forum, Jasola District Centre, New Delhi – 110025, India

103 Penang Road, #05–06/07, Visioncrest Commercial, Singapore 238467

Cambridge University Press is part of Cambridge University Press & Assessment, a department of the University of Cambridge.

We share the University's mission to contribute to society through the pursuit of education, learning and research at the highest international levels of excellence.

www.cambridge.org
Information on this title: www.cambridge.org/9781009618380

DOI: 10.1017/9781108529631

© Marius Stan 2025

This publication is in copyright. Subject to statutory exception and to the provisions of relevant collective licensing agreements no reproduction of any part may take place without the written permission of Cambridge University Press & Assessment.

When citing this work, please include a reference to the DOI 10.1017/9781108529631

First published 2025

A catalogue record for this publication is available from the British Library

ISBN 978-1-009-61838-0 Hardback
ISBN 978-1-108-43857-5 Paperback
ISSN 2397-9461 (online)
ISSN 2514-3824 (print)

Cambridge University Press & Assessment has no responsibility for the persistence or accuracy of URLs for external or third-party internet websites referred to in this publication and does not guarantee that any content on such websites is, or will remain, accurate or appropriate.

Kant's Natural Philosophy

Elements in the Philosophy of Immanuel Kant

DOI: 10.1017/9781108529631
First published online: August 2025

Marius Stan
Boston College

Author for correspondence: Marius Stan, marius.c.stan@gmail.com

Abstract: This Element analyzes Kant's metaphysics and epistemology of the exact science of nature. It explains his theory of true motion and ontology of matter. In addition, it reconstructs the patterns of evidential reasoning behind Kant's foundational doctrines.

Keywords: Kant, Newton, matter theory, mathematization of nature, space and time

© Marius Stan 2025

ISBNs: 9781009618380 (HB), 9781108438575 (PB), 9781108529631 (OC)
ISSNs: 2397-9461 (online), 2514-3824 (print)

Contents

Introduction	1
Metaphysics, I: Motion	4
Metaphysics, II: Matter	19
Epistemology	41
Conclusions	63
Appendices	65
Bibliography	71

uxori Carae, cuius amor sensum omnem exsuperat

Kant's Natural Philosophy

Introduction

This is a study of Kant's doctrine of laws, matter, motion, quantification, and their epistemology.

He wrote on these themes into the late Enlightenment, but they were quite old – they go back to Descartes' 1644 *Principles of Philosophy*. That book inaugurated a program of research, and a conceptual framework for it, that aimed to replace Aristotle. The Cartesian program rested on a few commitments that most figures then saw as nonnegotiable, on pain of regressing to the premodern world.

First, natural science must be anchored in a theory of *matter*: an account of its nature, primitive causal powers, and generic modes of action. Second, it required a theory of *motion*: a philosophical analysis of the motion species that science (mechanics, really) singles out for exact treatment. Third, the genuine science of nature is *quantitative*: it results from applying the various branches of mathematics to the behavior of matter in motion. Fourth, that science was based on *laws*: universal principles (of matter in motion) that govern all of nature inexorably and determine its states at every instant. Lastly, proper science must rest on a basis that has the greatest *evidence* this side of first philosophy. After 1700, consensus on these five commitments was practically universal. For Kant it would have counted as the received view.

However, agreement on these commitments went hand in hand with much dissent about the details of making good on them. There was protracted discussion about the real nature of body, the ontology of true motion, and the status of fundamental laws; the application of mathematics to nature; and the epistemology of exact science – its sources of evidence and patterns of confirmation.[1]

And so, his engagement with these commitments frames my account in this Element. I present and assess his metaphysics of matter and motion, his picture of how mathematics applies to them, and the epistemology behind his doctrines. For reasons of space, I leave out of account the fifth commitment (laws of nature), which Watkins 2019 has treated exhaustively.

Against this backdrop, I defend four theses. On the issue of true motion, Kant was a *relationist*: He analyzed motion as a special relation of body to other bodies, not to space. On the nature of *matter*, he changed his mind radically: from a discrete picture to a theory of matter as continuous. In regard to *quantification*, he relied tacitly on certain empirical premises, whose place in metaphysics is uncertain. His *epistemology* of foundations for exact science was

---

[1] Shabel 2005 is a lucid survey of the applicability of mathematics as an early modern theme. For Kant's relationist stance about motion, see also Messina 2018. For the other themes, see Brading and Stan 2023.

quite diverse: He used patterns of a priori inference that go well beyond his canon of transcendental argument.

Quantification deserves special notice here. From his natural philosophy, it is the part we know least well, but also the most problematic, or so I argue. In particular, he has two problems. His preferred representational framework for science – geometric concepts and methods – is too weak for the task it had to discharge. And, his quantitative pictures of matter and motion are in tension; they do not fit smoothly together.

Territory

My title hints at a broad range, but this Element treats just the main parts of Kant's doctrine. He defended them in three canonical texts, which I survey in brief now, with their titles serviceably abridged as *Monads, Motion*, and *Foundations*. The first two are youthful papers from the 1750s, and the last is a medium-sized tract from 1786.[2]

Officially, *Monads* deals with a problem in metaphysics. Genuine substance must be 'simple,' or partless, hence not divisible. Material substance, however, is in space, which is divisible to infinity. Then so is material substance, and so its concept appears incoherent. Kant solves this conundrum elegantly, by finding a type of substance that is partless, extended, and yet indivisible, conceptually not just physically. He calls it the 'physical monad,' an entity at the core of a powerful, versatile theory of matter. I explain its makeup and how it solves his problem in Section 2.

Motion solves another puzzle in metaphysics. Many then took causal action to reduce to collision, or impact. Now in collision, one body gains as much motion as the other loses. Impact thus seems to consist in a communication of motion, and many philosophers called it as such. Still, that cannot be literally true: Motion is a property (of some moving body), and properties cannot migrate from one substance to another. Kant again finds a solution. He argues for a theory of motion as a mutual relation between interacting bodies. From it, he explains impact as being a 'conflict' of forces, not a (metaphysically absurd) transfer of attributes.[3]

---

[2] Their full titles are *The Employment in Natural Philosophy of Metaphysics combined with Geometry, of which Sample I contains the Physical Monadology* (1756); *New Doctrine of Motion and Rest* (1758); and *Metaphysical Foundations of Natural Science*. Details and translations are in Kant 1992: 51–66, Kant 2012: 396–408, and Kant 2004. Hereafter, numbers from 467 to 567 refer to page numbers in volume IV of Kant 1903–. For the rest, I follow convention and cite Kant by volume and page number in the Academy's edition.

[3] Brading & Stan 2023 present exhaustively the background and Kant's solution to the problem of collisions.

He reprised both themes in his mature opus, *Foundations*, a four-chapter account that he called synonymously 'general doctrine of body' and 'rational physics.' Each chapter expounds the metaphysical foundations of a subdiscipline: 'phoronomy,' 'dynamics,' 'mechanics,' and 'phenomenology.' In real English, they denote respectively: a geometric kinematics of particle translation, a picture of matter, a theory of particle interactions, and a concept of objective motion. To keep my account fluent, I introduce here more terminology as follows. By *'Phoronomy'* I mean his chapter "Metaphysical Foundations of Phoronomy," and by 'Phoronomy' the discipline that he so denoted; *mutatis mutandis* for the other three parts of *Foundations*.

Kant kept reflecting on natural philosophy throughout the 1790s, in unpublished fragments nowadays called *Opus postumum*. Apparently, his views evolved so much that some exegetes speak of a 'post-Critical' Kant. I leave the *Opus* out of account here, which Stephen Howard recently clarified with much skill.[4]

Achievements

Kant's mature natural philosophy stands out from the respective doctrines of his predecessors. Unlike them, his grounding is *comprehensive*, because he worked out detailed pictures for all the key components of a philosophical basis for the science of nature: matter, motion, laws of nature, and mathematization. In the period between Galileo and the Late Enlightenment, Kant's foundational project exceeds all others in scope. And, there is a great deal of *unity* to his resulting picture, overall. In line with his transcendental approach, that unity depends on two sources: space and time qua sensible forms, and the twelve categories as concepts for all physical knowledge.

Space is a source of unity in two ways. First, all physical objects are 'in' space: They take up places, which are proper parts of space as a whole; and they are connected to each other by a metric relation, that is, relative distance. Second, space as *Ganzheitsform* ensures that all objects have certain spatial features: size, shape, position, and the space curves they describe as they move. Hence, geometry – the science of space – ipso facto applies to all objects. In effect, space being a form (of sense) entails that we can have geometric knowledge, quantitative and exact, of every material body we may encounter in sensible experience. As to the categories, the four groups, or headings, into which Kant grouped them guarantee that all objects have certain generic properties: quantitative, qualitative, and relational. And, the modal categories unify the motion behaviors of all bodies. They justify a research program aimed

---

[4] See Howard 2023. For the long-term reception of Kant's *Opus*, see Basile 2013.

at referring their individual motion-states to a single descriptive standard: absolute space as Kant means it.

This strategy yielded a picture (of physical knowledge and its metaphysics) that is considerably unified. At the same time, deep below the surface of that picture lie certain *tensions*. By that I mean descriptive mismatches, not logical contradictions. One tension is between his laws of motion and his matter theory. The laws are fit for discrete particles, whereas Kant thinks that matter is continuous, not discrete. Another tension is between descriptive language and the needs of quantitative theory. He believed that exact science must use the concepts and methods of synthetic geometry; but mathematized mechanics in his time had come to require a different descriptive framework, built from algebraic resources. We must not fault him for those tensions. Virtually everyone then who tried to ground physical science in a theory of matter *and also* in general laws of motion ended up with significant tensions in their foundational picture. In fact, to this day it is not clear that we *can* have a unified foundation for all classical mechanics.[5]

I suggest a genetic explanation for his tensions. In the Critical decade, Kant *recycled* crucial doctrines from his philosophical youth. He took those doctrines and sought to retrofit them to a conceptual architectonic supplied by the First Critique.[6] But in the 1750s he had not checked that his doctrines were mutually compatible; and in the 1780s his chief priority was to unify them from the outside, as it were – by way of his categories – not to check them for internal compatibility. In the long run, however, it turns out that his mature doctrines were not entirely compatible, their outer appearance of unity notwithstanding. I hope my longer expositions below will lend more plausibility to this conjecture.

Metaphysics, I: Motion

Many early moderns believed the new science requires the foundational premise that bodies have certain states of motion that count as privileged, or theoretically distinguished. Often, that privileged state was called 'true motion.' Kant agreed with them. Accordingly, in the 1750s, he developed his own theory of true motion, which he then reworked in his maturity. Before I survey it, a few words about why he needed one.

---

[5] On the first tension, see Stan 2014; on the second, cf. Stan (in press). For discussion of the general problem, see Brading & Stan 2023.

[6] The four most important pre-Critical doctrines are: that matter has two essential forces (attractive and repulsive); that two laws of motion (inertia and the action-reaction principle) are a priori and explanatorily privileged; that action by contact (collision) requires grounding from these two laws; and that true motion is a privileged relation between interacting bodies.

True Motion

Start with an intuitive distinction. To an observer, a body may *appear* to move or rest; but we may ask whether it really, or *truly*, does move or rest at that instant. Natural philosophers took it for granted that, for any single body, there is a fact about its true state of motion: It either really moves or really rests, but not both at the same time. Whoever grants that apparent/true motion is a valid distinction then faced a hard problem: What is the nature of true motion? What does it consist in?

At the time, they ran into this problem on three strategic fronts. First was the heliocentrism debate. Both Ptolemaists and Copernicans granted that the sun *appears* to move, and the earth to rest. The debate was whether our globe *truly* moves, despite appearing to rest; *mutatis mutandis* for the sun. Second, the new science of the 1600s rested on a key principle, the Law of Inertia. However, the law – and all basic laws of mechanics, for that matter – makes a claim about the true motion of bodies. In regard to merely apparent motions, the law is trivially false.[7] Third, to usher in the new science of nature, philosophers had argued for a sparse ground-level ontology comprising just 'matter' and 'motion.' Kant did too, as he claimed that motion is the "fundamental determination of anything that is to be an object of outer sense" (476). If we read on, we realize that he meant *true* motion, just like his predecessors.

So much for motivations. Now, what is a theory of motion? Briefly, it is an account of its metaphysical nature; a philosophical doctrine of what true motion *consists* in. From Descartes to our times, these theories have been versions of two broad, irreconcilable metaphysics. One is Absolutism, the doctrine that true motion is change of place in Absolute Space, an immaterial, infinite container-like entity. The other is Relationism, which takes true motion to consist in a privileged, explanatorily distinguished relation to some *material* setup. The specific difference of each variant is the particular setup, or frame, that it privileges. Next, I must remove a source of deep confusion. The term 'relative motion' is radically equivocal; it has two distinct senses, and they are logical contraries – they do not overlap at all. At the time, there were two distinct doctrines built around these two contrary senses. Relativism: motion is relative = bodies have *no* true motions. Their kinematic relations to other bodies are on a par; none is privileged, or 'true.' Relationism: motion is relative = each body

---

[7] Galileo knew (and then Euler proved) that cannonballs shot along the local meridian deviate westward; and yet the horizontal component of their motion is inertial, so it should follow the meridian's north–south line, with no deviation. Newton knew that objects dropped from rest deviate eastward, even though the only force on them is *downward*, due to gravity. Of course, these violations of the law are just apparent; the reason why the law of inertia seems falsified is that the earth (to which these motions are referred) is not a true inertial frame, because it spins.

has one *true* motion, consisting in a relation to a *material* frame; it is not a motion in Absolute Space.

Without clarity on this term, a reader may think that Kant flatly contradicts himself by claiming that all motion is relative, and also that motion in absolute space exists. He does not contradict himself, as I explain shortly. Moreover, avoiding the equivocation above helps us place him correctly on the map of early modern views: He really belongs in the same camp as Descartes, Berkeley, and (sometimes) Leibniz. That is, Kant was always a relationist – and his misleading appeal to 'absolute space' in *Foundations* only obscures that fact. He first articulated his relationism in the 1750s, well before the Critical turn. In *Motion*, he sets out by dismissing Absolute Space out of hand, and then decrees bluntly:

> there is something lacking in the expressions "motion" and "rest." I should never use them in an absolute sense, but always respectively [*respective*]. I should never say a body rests, without adding with respect to which things it is at rest; and never say that it moves, without at the same time naming the objects in respect to which it changes its relation. (2: 17)

So far, Kant has just declared motion *in general* to consist in a kinematic relation. Evidently then, a body c has as many motions as there are bodies relative to which c changes position over time.[8] Still, Kant agrees that each body has a true motion, *wahrhafte Bewegung*, and so he must explain cogently which one of c's many relations counts as its true motion. Kant decides that it is the relation of approach (or receding) to the particular body d that interacts with c at that instant; and that it is a "mutual" relation. That is, d truly moves relative to c just as much: "Must we not ascribe the motion to both, namely in equal measure? Their mutual approach may be ascribed to the one just as much as to the other" (2: 18).

Why is *that* relation privileged? Because it is causally efficient, he explains: As c moves relative to d, it is able to thereby cause a change in d's state; for instance, by colliding with it. And, to ask about true motion is to inquire "about the action that the two bodies exert on each other" (2: 18f.). Then he ends with an account of the quantity of true motion. It is the speed s (between c and d) such that the true speeds of c and d are inversely proportional to their masses. In a modern paraphrase, the early Kant takes true motion to be a relation T obtaining between any two interacting bodies c, d. Absent their interaction, T is not well defined; T is symmetric and supervenes on two relational properties

---

[8] In our terms, Kant takes motion to be a dyadic predicate xRy, where x and y are variables ranging over bodies. Then a body c has n motions, where $(n-1)$ is the number of actual bodies at any time t.

C, D of c and d, respectively. Numerically, C and D are true speeds, measured in the mass-center frame of the system $c+d$.[9]

The Critical Years

Kant was remarkably conservative about his early relationism. Its core survived intact into the 1780s, as did his broad strategy to establish it. First, a word about its framing. In the Critical years, he called that view 'phenomenology,' and expounded it in the last chapter of *Foundations*. The term is technical; his Phenomenology is a theory of true motion, its species, and the method for inferring to it from merely apparent motion (and rest) as given to the senses.[10]

Recall that the young Kant justified his theory by a three-step case: (1) reject Absolute Space as a candidate *explanans*, (2) argue that motion *generaliter* is a direct relation between bodies, then (3) for any body, single out one relation as its true motion. The steps are visible in his mature view as well. Kant again sets out by dismissing Newton's container: "qua non-material, it cannot be an object of experience ... Absolute space is thus *in itself* nothing" (481). With it out of the way, Kant moves to affirm that motion consists in a relation between material entities: "As object of experience, all motion is just relative. And, the space in which we perceive it is a relative [empirical] space as well ... All motion and rest is relative, and cannot be absolute. I.e., we can think matter to move solely relative to matter, never relative to mere space void of matter" (481, 559).

That is, any object appears to move always relative to some other object. Hence, knowing that it *truly* moves also involves referring its motion to some privileged 'matter,' or physical setup. This claim needs argument, of course. He does have one, spanning much of *Phenomenology*; it is the very argument for the general view that each body has one *true* motion.

At this juncture, the Critical framework becomes explanatorily relevant, as his categories begin to drive the account. That is because Phenomenology deals with true – as opposed to apparent – motion, and while the latter is just given to the senses, the former is the object of considered judgment, which needs a category structure to be deployed:

> Like all else represented by the senses, motion is given only as appearance. For its representation to become experience, it is further required that something be thought by the understanding. Namely, beside the manner of the representation inhering in the *subject*, we must also think the determination of

---

[9] For context, justification, and significance see Friedman 2013 and Stan 2009.
[10] Kant took the term from Lambert but changed its intended application; see the discussion in Friedman 2013: 421–30.

an *object* through it. Hence, the movable becomes an object of experience qua movable when an *object* (here, a material thing) is thought as *determined* in respect to the *predicate* of motion. (554; original emphasis)

In particular, the categories of *modality* yield both a taxonomy of true motions and also the *differentia specifica* for each of the three species in it: true motion is either possible or actual or necessary. Specifically, straight-line motion is possible, circular motion (rotation) is actual, and linear acceleration (from interactions) is necessary.

Let us begin with possible motion; it helps here to put his point in modern terms first. Recall that Kant defines Phenomenology as the discipline of moving matter qua possible object of experience, that is, of theory-embedded knowledge. Moreover, his categories of modality are epistemic – they denote the *strength of the evidence* available for some modally qualified knowledge claim. So, in calling rectilinear motion 'possible,' Kant means: for any claim that body B has velocity v relative to frame **V**, we may substitute the claim that B has w relative to **W**; and no evidence from mechanics could show v to be more likely than w. That seems to be the tenor of his words that (bearing in mind that his 'relative-' and 'absolute space' are material frames):

> in experience – or knowledge that determines the object validly for all appearances – there is *not the slightest difference* between the motion of a body in relative space and the body's rest in absolute space while the relative one moves at the same speed but in the opposite direction ... That is, through the concept of motion as object of experience, it is in itself underdetermined – hence *equally valid* – whether a body is represented as moving in relative space; or we represent the space as in motion relative to the subject. Now that which is itself undetermined in regard to two mutually opposed predicates is thereby *merely possible*. (556–7; my emphasis)

On my reading, then, Kant's concept 'possible motion' is his answer to Galilean relativity, a form of underdetermination in mechanics.[11]

He then moves to argue that rotation is its own species of motion; I treat it separately, just below; now I explain his account of necessary motions. They obtain in contexts in which bodies are 'movent,' that is, causally active by displacing other bodies, thereby setting them in motion; in our terms, movents impart momentum to

---

[11] Galilean relativity is an outcome of the laws of classical mechanics. It has to do with the fact that, by applying the laws to apparent motions (given by observation and experiment on any mechanical system) no true *velocity* can be inferred or computed. Thus the appearances underdetermine the experience (qua theory-mediated knowledge) of bodies' true velocities. For that reason, it is *possible* – in the sense of permitted by mechanical theory – to assign to them any initial velocity before we apply the laws to infer the bodies' future motions. (All these assignments are, of course, relative to a choice of inertial frame.) This was known in Kant's time; for conclusive evidence, see Euler 1765, chapter I, VI.

other bodies. This generic process is 'mutual,' or symmetric: "any *active* relation of matters *in space* – and all change in relation, so far as they can be *causes* of action – we must always regard as mutual" (545; italics in original). So, movents are simply bodies in interactions. As an official example for analysis, Kant gives contact action, specifically collision. Still, with some interpretive freedom it seems that his points carry over to action-at-a-distance forces too.[12]

Kant's concept raises two philosophical questions. First, what makes this aspect of interaction a species of *true* motion? On this issue, he is clear and conservative. Recall his youthful idea that all motion is a material relation, and for each body one motion-relation is privileged on causal grounds. In *Foundations* he reprises that thought: "All *active* relations of matters *in space* – and also all changes of these relations, insofar as they may be *causes* of certain actions or effects – must always be represented as mutual" (545). Ergo, when an interaction obtains, each body in it has a true motion relative to the co-involved bodies. Second, in what sense are these true motions necessary? Prima facie, it is because Kant claims that objective experience of these motions counts as necessary knowledge. But if we ask what sort of necessity they have, the truth is that he really seems undecided; and current exegesis reflects his ambivalence. Some take it to be *physical* necessity: corporeal action is constrained by Kant's Third Law, a principle that requires all kinematic effects to come in pairs. Namely, when a body C causes a motion-change in D, then C too suffers a motion-change caused by D. He suggests as much: "by the Third Law of Mechanics, the communication of motion is possible only through the community of their originally-moving forces. And, this community is possible only through mutually-opposed and equal motion" (545). Others take it to be *conceptual* necessity: Kant establishes his claim – that interacting bodies necessarily have unique true motions – by conceptual analysis of the concept of a body moving relative to another as they interact. This too has textual support: "and this follows from mere concepts of a relative motion ... Because of that, it is (like everything sufficiently provable from mere concepts) a law of simply necessary counter-motion" (558, 562). Kant encourages both these readings in the same breath – a brief paragraph, too pithy and obscure for such a crucial topic.[13]

Rotation

At last, I move to a very difficult problem. Accounting for it adequately is the acid test for Kant's doctrine of absolute space, and failing in this task would weaken that doctrine considerably. Next, I explain the problem and his solution, then I end with a critical look at it.

---

[12] The clearest, strongest case for that is Friedman 2013: 353–9.
[13] The first interpretation is in Friedman 2013: 560–2; for the second, see Stan 2013.

Context

Kant's account of rotation is easier to grasp if we look at it against a historical backdrop. That foil is Newton's critique of Descartes. In *Principles of Philosophy*, Descartes gave a doctrine of true motion, which he defined as a change in a body's metric relations to other bodies that immediately surround it. Newton in *Principia* then showed that Descartes' definition was inadequate, because (inter alia) it failed to make sense of rotation. In a Scholium to the Definitions, Newton proved Descartes wrong in an empirical setting, with a mass of water set in circular motion. Newton took it for granted that we have physical criteria for telling whether the water really rotates or not. He then explained that, based on Descartes' definition, water counts as truly rotating when, in fact, it is physically at rest; and it counts as truly at rest when, in fact, it shows the physical signs of true rotation.[14] Thus, Descartes' definition of true motion *anti-correlates* with the physical behavior of material objects; hence, a science based on that definition will *eo ipso* be inadequate. In contrast, Newton's own definition – absolutism, or the view that true motion consists in change of place in Absolute Space – always correlates, infallibly, with the physical behavior of bodies that happen to be truly rotating. In sum, absolutism gets it right on physical grounds, whereas Descartes' version of relationism gets it wrong. And so, any other species of relationist doctrine must ensure that it correlates adequately with the physical behavior of bodies in true spin motion. My critical discussion below (of Kant's analysis of rotation) takes Newton's lesson to heart and spells out its quantitative details.

Finally, a note of caution. In Newton's Scholium, circular motion – spin – shows up twice, in two different contexts, and for different purposes. One is the bucket experiment just described. The other is a *thought* experiment known as the 'rotating globes scenario.' Newton used the former to make a point in metaphysics, namely, that Descartes' definition of true motion is inadequate, whereas his own definition *is* adequate. Additionally, he used the latter to make a point in

---

[14] That setup became known as the 'bucket experiment.' In a bucket suspended from a rope twisted tight, Newton puts water and lets it settle until its free surface was even; then he lets go of the bucket, which begins to spin, turned by the rope now free to unwind. From then on, the water goes through three stages of behavior that matter for the philosophical issue at hand. Stage 1: the water and the bucket are in relative motion – the bucket's inner wall slides past the water particles next to it. And yet, for a short while the water's surface remains even. That is physical evidence for the water being then truly at rest, and yet in motion relative to the bucket. Stage 2: friction forces (exerted by the spinning bucket) drag the water in contact with it along as the bucket spins. The water's free surface slowly begins to curve into a concave shape. That is physical evidence for the water entering a state of true spin. Stage 3: the water reaches maximum concavity (it has risen up against the bucket walls to the maximum height). It is physical evidence that it has reached its maximum rate of *true rotation*. And yet, the water is *at rest* relative to the bucket: they spin at the same rate (with respect to an observer at rest in space).

epistemology, namely, that we can have knowledge of true rotation (its quantity and direction) even *without* evidence from any *actual* change between bodies.[15] Kant explicitly acknowledged just Newton's second case (the rotating-globes scenario), and never discussed the first. Below, I do that on his behalf.

True Spin

Consider two descriptions of apparent motions happening at the same time. (1) Emily sits on the earth and looks at the stars, from dusk to dawn. Over hours, the stars as a whole appear to spin around her location. (2) Jack sits on Alpha Centauri and looks toward Emily. Over hours, she appears to spin around the earth's axis.[16] Separately, Jack and Emily write down their individual observations in quantitative terms, namely, as changes of angular distance over time (Figure 1).

As descriptions of *apparent* motion, the two are equivalent: neither contains any kinematic quantity that the other does not. However, from Copernicus to Kant everyone thought there *is* a difference between (1) and (2). Namely, one of the two systems *truly* and *really* spins, whereas the other just *seems* to spin, but does not really do so; in reality, it does not rotate at all.[17] And, Huygens and Newton had taught how to detect true spin – by means of dynamical criteria, due to force-like effects present when true spin occurs, but absent in cases of merely apparent spin.[18] In sum, after 1673 there was universal consensus that true spin and apparent spin are genuinely distinct states, even though they are kinematically equivalent; and we can tell the difference by means of objective facts.

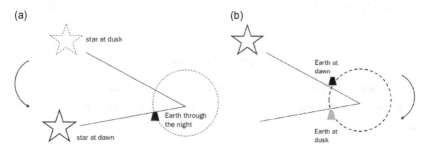

Figure 1 The same apparent rotation (viz. finite angular displacement) as observed from two Kantian 'relative spaces.'

---

[15] For lucid philosophical analysis, see Rynasiewicz 1995.
[16] Rotation is a species of circular motion around some axis. When the axis is internal to the moving system, the motion is often called 'spin.'
[17] That was the crux of the Copernican controversy: whether the stars truly revolve around us or just seem to do so; and whether the earth truly spins or is at rest.
[18] In the seventeenth century, ascertaining that true spin occurs relied on what we call pseudo-inertial effects, viz. on accelerations due to something other than genuine forces. (Here, 'genuine' denotes forces that are seated in bodies and obey Newton's third law, i.e., they come

Still, agreement that true spin is a real state put pressure on natural philosophers to answer a metaphysical question: what is the *nature* of true spin? What does it *consist* in? Just as with true motion, two schools of thought emerged as follows. Absolutism: true spin consists in circular motion with respect to an immaterial container, the Absolute Space of Newton and Euler. Relationism: true spin consists in motion relative to a privileged matter frame, or 'relative space.'

Now for a crucial aspect. Choosing a position had consequences and came with obligations. Specifically, Newton and Huygens had created theories that gave determinate quantitative answers to the following question: How *fast* and in what *direction* does a true-rotating body move? Answer: the speed of true spin equals $w^2 r$, where w is the angular velocity around the axis of rotation, and r is the distance to that axis. The direction of true spin is *tangential* to the trajectory at that point.[19] Their answer was sound and final – no one thought that it could be ignored or rejected.

Newton and Euler chose absolutism, which gave them an easy way to make sense of true spin. The formula is valid only when the spin is described from an inertial frame, and Absolute Space is one by design. In contrast, relationists faced enormous difficulties. There are many – very many – relative spaces such that, if the spin is referred to *them*, the formula becomes trivially false.[20] So, a responsible relationist must choose very carefully how she states her position, or else she runs afoul of true rotation. Specifically, she must solve two tasks: first, explain relative to which *material* frame spin counts as true motion; second, show that her relationist analysis *agrees* with the direction and quantity of true spin as given earlier. This is the background to Kant's account of rotation, easily the most difficult part of his *Phenomenology*. I turn to it now.

Kant on True Spin

In line with his general approach in Phenomenology, he accepts that true rotation is a genuine state of motion, and he assigns it a modal category, namely, actuality:

---

in pairs, are equal, and opposite.) Among those effects were 'centrifugal forces,' which act on the line of gravity (vertically) but opposite to it; and Coriolis effects, which lead free-falling bodies to deviate eastward. Huygens had quantified the strength of centrifugal force. Newton knew that eastward deflection (in falling bodies) obtains, as did Kant. For details, see Stan 2015.

[19] Huygens announced these results in an appendix on 'centrifugal force,' placed at the end of his *Horologium oscillatorium* of 1673. Then, in 1728, 's Gravesande had published these results with proofs for them, as part of Huygens' *Opera reliqua*.

[20] That is, referring spin to most matter-frames yields the wrong predictions. Neither the actual direction nor the circular speed of bodies (as inferred from their centrifugal forces) conforms to the descriptions of the spin relative to such frames.

> Theorem II. The circular motion of a matter, as distinguished from the opposite motion of the space, is an *actual* predicate of it. But the opposite motion of a relative space, taken instead of the body's motion, is not an actual motion of the latter. Rather, if it is taken to be such, is mere illusion. (536)

Saying 'is an actual motion' means we have conclusive evidence that some bodies are in true spin; and by 'illusion' he means that, based on the evidence, the judgment 'this relative space really rotates' is false.

Behind his thought are situations like the two observers mentioned earlier. The same kinematic content (viz., angular motion) can be described as the body spinning relative to the matter-frame where Jack sits; or as a motion of his frame around the body on which Emily sits. In classical physics, evidence from centrifugal effects shows that Emily spins truly and Jack does not. Kant's theorem codifies just that kind of univocal ascription of true spin motion.

Now he faces up to a hard problem. Often, we can establish true spin from facts that make *no* reference to an external frame, and involve no kinematic relation to it. In fact, we could prove the actual existence of true spin even if no external frame *exists* at all; and Kant knows it.[21] That puts tremendous pressure on his relationism about rotation; here is why:

1. Some bodies are in states of true spin. [the early modern consensus]
2. True spin consists in *actual* kinematic change relative to an *external* frame. [by Kant's theorem II of Phenomenology]
3. We can establish that a thing spins truly even though *no* actual change obtains relative to an *external* frame. [cf. Kant's falling-stone scenario]
4. Conclusion: Theorem II is false.

Then what does true rotation *consist* in? What is the nature of objective circular motion? He realizes the gravity of his situation: "So, a motion – which is a change of external relations in space – can be given empirically, even though this space is not itself given, and is no object of experience. This is a paradox deserving to be solved" (558).

Now for Kant's solution. To explain it well, I must introduce two concepts; they are implicit in his treatment of true spin. One concept is 'opposite parts' (see Figure 2).

In a body or system *K* in true spin, any two matter bits count as opposite parts if they lie in the same plane, diametrically across from each other, normal to the axis of spin. The other concept is 'latent motion,' which I explicate thus:

---

[21] That is the point of Kant's falling-stone scenario in *Phenomenology* (557–8). The stone gets deflected (eastward), and that is evidence that the earth spins truly. And yet, establishing this fact did *not* rely on referring the earth's motion to the stars, the sun, or any external frame at all. For complete details, see Stan 2015.

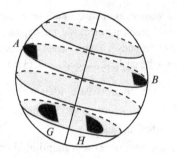 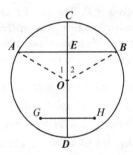

Figure 2 In a system that spins, any two pieces of matter lying in the same plane, equidistant from the axis of rotation, count as 'opposite parts' in Kant's sense. For instance, *A* and *B*; or *G* and *H*. In his analysis, true rotation consists in opposite parts (latently) moving relative to each other.

- If two matter bits are *actually* at mutual *rest*, but they *would* move relative to each other, provided the forces between them were counterfactually turned off, then the bits are in latent motion.
- But, if they would keep the same relative distance (even with the forces turned off), the bits are at latent rest.

The concept of latent motion is not Kant's explicit phrase; it is my term. Still, it makes good sense of his answer to the 'paradox' of rotation, which he gives in a General Remark to Phenomenology. In essence, I construe his solution as follows. True spin consists in latent motion, which is a relation of matter to matter. Namely, if a system rotates truly, its 'opposite parts' are in latent motion relative to *each other*, pairwise. That is my reconstruction of Kant's difficult train of thought behind his official resolution of the 'paradox' of true spin.

> Though spin is *no change* of relations to an *empirical* space, yet it is not an absolute motion. Rather, it is a continual change of matters' relations *to each other*, although we represent this change in absolute space. Thus, it is really just *relative* motion – and so, on account of that, is true motion [*wahr*]. This claim relies on representing the *mutual*, continual *receding* of any two opposite parts *from each other*. For this motion is real in absolute space. (561 f)

But if a system appears to spin and yet its parts are not in latent motion, it displays the 'illusion' of rotation, though it really is at rotational rest.

Assessment

Before we evaluate for soundness Kant's treatment of rotation, recall his basic commitment, as a relationist: All true motion is a privileged relation to matter.

Kant's Natural Philosophy

There are four assumptions behind this thesis. Actuality: All true motion consists in an *actual* change of kinematic relations. Frame-dependence: True motion is always a relation to a relative *space*, or matter frame. Externality: All true motion is relative to a material space that is *external* to the moving body. Cognizability: True motion is knowable *only* as a relation of the body to a material space. For motion to be given "even as appearance, we need an empirical representation of the space relative to which the mobile must change its relation," or else it is not a cognizing of a *motion* (559).

Now these commitments extend to rotation: it too amounts to a "change of external relations in space." But his grappling with the 'paradox' of true spin strains them to the breaking point. In particular, his official solution requires him to quietly violate all of these commitments, as follows. Not every true motion is an actual change of relations: True spin is not actual, just latent. Not all true motion is a relation to a space: Some are relations of bodies to bodies, for example, true spin (and action by contact too). Not every motion is an external relation of the body, to another matter: True spin is *internal* to the body, qua relation between its parts. Not all true motion requires a sensible-material space for us to relate it to: True spin is cognizable even when *no* such space is given in experience (Figure 3).

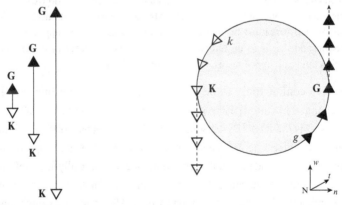

Figure 3 (left) The latent motion of two parts K, G of a spinning body as Kant analyzes it. The parts' mutual distance would grow if the physical bond that holds them were dissolved. The increase would be along the straight line between them, and nonuniform. (It is a quadratic function of time.) Note that the latent-moving parts do not form an angle with each other, so it is meaningless to speak of their motion having an angular speed. (right) The motion of the two parts K and G as seen from a true inertial frame N*wtn* or by an observer at rest in Newton's Absolute Space.

Even evaluated more narrowly, his treatment of rotation falters not a little. Recall that a condition of adequacy for any analysis of rotation was that it vindicate the quantity and direction of true spin. But his analysis secures neither. For one, the quantity includes an angular speed, w. However, in the latent motion that Kant privileged in his analysis, the concept of a change of angle is not well defined: Opposite parts do not make an angle with each other. For another, true spin is tangent to the trajectory, whereas the direction of latent motion is perpendicular to the orbit (see Figure 3) – an unwelcome result.

In fairness, his mixed success is typical of early modern struggles to analyze rotation without resort to Absolute Space; since that challenge was so difficult, I gave it separate exposition here. Kant certainly did no worse than his fellow relationists on this count.[22] The broader question is, was it worth discarding Newton's space if the alternative is so costly?

Absolute Space

Having defended a brand of relationism (the view of true motion *qua* relation to *matter*, not to immaterial space) Kant at the eleventh hour seems to turn around and reach for absolute space:

> three concepts are absolutely *indispensable* for general natural science ... Their *common basis* is the concept of absolute space. But how do we come to this peculiar concept? And on what rests the *necessity* of its use? ... All motion and rest must be reduced to absolute space, if the appearance of motion and rest is to be turned into a determinate concept of experience, which unites all appearances. (559–60; my emphasis)

This is very confounding, to be sure.[23] Is he contradicting himself? Has he quietly changed his mind? Is he giving new meanings to old words?

I suggest it is the latter. By 'absolute space' Kant means a different thing from Newton and Euler's term. Their phrase denoted Absolute Space, that is, a nonmaterial, mind-independent, rigid, immobile, dynamically inert infinite container for all bodies. Kant called their entity "transcendentally real," to signal that it counts as unknowable in light of the First Critique. He made *his* absolute space safe for transcendental idealism, by having it always denote a *representation*. A complex one, semantically and pragmatically; he uses 'absolute space' in three regimes:

- phoronomic – absolute space is the concept of a material frame that we may suppose stationary, introducible at will so as to redescribe the kinematics of some system of mobile points (hence of matter particles).

---

[22] For a critical survey of his predecessors' attempts, see Chapter VII in Earman 1989.
[23] So confounding, that for about two centuries no real attempt was made to explain it. At long last Friedman 1992 set the modern standard.

- phenomenologic – absolute space is the concept of a frame, arbitrarily large, with the origin at the mass-center of the physical world.
- regulative – absolute space is an idea of reason, namely, a twin imperative: Regard any material frame as *just* a temporary descriptive support for the motions of bodies; and require theorists to seek ever larger frames, more likely to be inertial.

I take these senses to be natural readings of Kant's difficult words about it. For the first semantic regime:

> Absolute space denotes every other *relative* space that I can always *think* for myself outside the given relative space, and extend to infinity beyond the given one. That is, I can *think* it as enclosing the latter, and can *assume* the latter to move inside it. This enlarged space is always a *material* one. Still, as I have it only *in thought*, and know nothing about the matter that designates it, I thus abstract from this matter. So, this space is *represented* as a pure, non-empirical, and absolute space. I can compare every empirical space with it, and represent the empirical as movable inside it. Hence it counts as itself immobile." (481 f; my emphasis)

For the second: "Hence we must think an absolute space to which all relative motions can be referred – one in which everything empirical is movable." And for the third: "[absolute space] is a necessary concept of reason – hence nothing but a mere idea ... that ought to serve as a rule for regarding all motion in absolute space as merely relative" (559, 560).

How do his three aspects fit together? Kant has an answer, but it is complex and demanding. No amount of summarizing could do it justice, but here is an attempt. For ease of exposition, I refer to his three aspects of absolute space (qua representation, not immaterial container) as the 'phoronomic frame,' the 'regulative frame,' and the 'phenomenologic frame,' respectively. I base the following account on Michael Friedman's work; the ideas are his, though rephrased in my terms.

There are two sciences that need a notion of absolute space, or frame of reference that counts as privileged: mechanics and physical astronomy.[24] Research in these two areas – coming to know the true motions of bodies – is a temporally extended process. Really, it is open-ended and reaches into the future. As Friedman sees it, this diachronic process has stages and is subject to certain rules. Kant's absolute space concerns these stages and rules, as follows.

In the early stages, we take the earth as the *phoronomic* frame. We regard it as being at rest, and refer the motions of bodies we investigate – objects above ground, planets as observed in astronomy – to the earth. For two reasons,

---
[24] The theory that bridges these two disciplines is celestial mechanics, which after 1740 was often called 'mechanical astronomy.'

however, this stage is insufficient. One, we know the earth is not really immobile; it could be moving (relative to some other material frame), a possibility which must be investigated. Two, it is a somewhat deficient frame: When we refer observed motions to it, they differ from what we should expect based on the laws of motion.[25] In consequence, *regulative* absolute space demands we move beyond this stage (of using the earth as our phoronomic frame). This regulative demand has two aspects. We use it as a *negative* condition: We prohibit researchers from regarding any matter frame as sufficient for all inquiry; no ascriptions of corporeal motion relative to that frame counts as the body's true motion. And we adopt it as a positive heuristic: We require researchers to keep looking for matter frames that come closer and closer to the key feature of absolute space, namely, permanent rest.[26]

Accordingly, we move to another stage in the process: We choose another 'matter' as the new frame, or phoronomic absolute space. Friedman argues this frame (its origin, really) is located at the mass center of the solar system. This choice of reference is better than the previous one: Observed motions better agree with predictions from the laws of mechanics and astronomy. Still, the same considerations as above apply at this stage as well. And so, regulative absolute space demands that we progress to yet another stage. We choose another, even better phoronomic frame, for example, one located at the mass center of the Milky Way galaxy. (Kant's picture of the physical universe was expansive, generous, and rich in structure at every scale.)

In principle, this process is open-ended. After all, the regulative demands will apply at every future stage, though with less and less stringency. When we survey our progress through these stages, we begin to see (in thought, of course; we *infer* to it) an endpoint to this collective advance. At that final stage lies *phenomenologic* absolute space: a frame that no longer counts as possibly in motion, and relative to which all observed motions agree with the motions predicted from theory. Admittedly, epistemic access to that frame lies at the end of inquiry, as it were. Phenomenologic absolute space is not given in the appearance: We do not perceive it, and no relative space has any sensible marks that single it out as absolute qua *truly* at rest. Thus we have to *make* it into an object of experience – by progressing through the stages I outlined, on Friedman's behalf.[27]

---

[25] For instance, relative to the earth, planets do not obey Kepler's Third Law, a corollary of Newton's laws in *Principia*; and, objects in free fall from great heights seem to deviate eastward, whereas the laws predict they should fall straight down.

[26] This explanatory capsule is really my analytic gloss on Friedman's exegesis of absolute space in Kant; cf. his 1992 and 2013: 413–21, 474–502.

[27] The relevant Kantian contrast here is between appearance and experience. Namely, between a sensed thing grasped by pre-theoretical perception; and an object known from theory, viz. complex inference mediated by a body of organized truths.

Lastly, if Kant displaced Newton's container space, then – for architectonic, foundational, and historical reasons – should he not have supplanted Absolute Time as well? Yes, he should; regrettably, he stayed silent on this matter. Still, there *are* hermeneutic projects to fill that gap for him. In fairness, these projects are incipient, and much work remains to be done.[28]

Metaphysics, II: Matter

After Descartes, philosophical grounding for the new science moved on two tracks: an ontology of motion, and a theory of matter. A full metaphysical foundation required both. We saw in Section I what Kant thought about the nature of motion. Here, I move to explain his matter theory. But first, a point of clarification.

Early modern matter theories aimed to answer two broad questions. One was about its *nature*.[29] For the post-Scholastics, the Aristotelian picture of matter would no longer do, and so they had to answer that question for themselves. Accounting for its nature required the philosopher to list the essential properties of matter, its generic causal *powers*, and its architecture at fundamental scales, namely, the geometric makeup and kinematic behaviors of the least bit of matter, or ultimate constituent of the bodies given in experience. The other question regarded its *quantification*. Post-Scholastic doctrines were radically novel in that they expected the essential properties of matter to be mathematizable, or represented as quantities.

Kant accepted this twin mandate and gave solutions to all the subsidiary tasks above. Now I examine his matter theory – from his youth to the Critical years – along two tracks of inquiry: the nature of matter and its mathematization. I examine some of his ways of gathering evidence for his doctrine of matter in Section IV.

First, I must clarify some notions. Kant has two terms, 'dynamics' and 'mechanics,' but they are nonstandard. His dynamics is really a theory of matter. He called it thus to signal he endorsed the Leibnizian tenet that force is 'original,' or essential to matter and irreducible to more basic attributes.

---

[28] Two related exegetic proposals for a Kantian analogue of Newton's absolute time are Friedman (2013: 62–7) and Stan 2019.

[29] This comprehensive ambition (and its broadly nonempirical sources of evidential support) distinguishes philosophical doctrines of matter from their empirical cousins, which are more circumscribed in explanatory scope and more tightly yoked to their relevant empirical phenomena. Consider the kinetic theory of matter, a 19th-century creation. It posits that, at fundamental scales, matter was made up of small, discrete volumes of mass, separated by large average distances, and endowed with momentum and kinetic energy. It aimed to account for relatively circumscribed phenomena, e.g., gas dynamics, heat flow, optical behaviors (refraction, polarization), and chemical bonding.

His mechanics is just a theory of actual motion-changes in free (unconstrained) bodies.[30]

Matter Theory in the 1750s

Kant spent some fifty years thinking through what we now call 'matter theory.' He reflected on the essential attributes of matter; the geometric makeup of body, its kinematic behaviors, and dynamical powers. In the 1780s, they become a part of the "general doctrine of body," his philosophical foundation for the science of material objects. As in Section I, I start with his earliest relevant output and end with some thoughts on quantification in his theory of matter.

Occasion

His first robust outline of a matter theory was *Monads*. To understand his aims and premises there, it helps to know his context. First, the Berlin Academy in the 1740s had been home to debates between defenders and opponents of 'monads,' a family of views claiming that genuine substance is a partless simple.[31] Second, there was a proof that space (qua entity for geometric theorizing) was infinitely divisible. The version that he knew was by John Keill, but there were others. Third, some prominent local figures had turned impenetrability into a basic, *irreducible* attribute of material substance. Some had even placed it below extension itself, in the order of grounding.[32] Fourth and last, Wolff and his school had split Leibniz's idealist legacy into a dual ontology that included 'elements,' a dis-mentalized species of substance. They were metaphysical simples with no representational powers at all, not even the *petites perceptions* of Leibniz's late doctrine. Having stripped them of all mindlike attributes, Wolff

---

[30] The standard senses for the two terms come out of work by d'Alembert and Euler in the 1740s and later. For them, mechanics was the general theory of impressed motion, with two main branches: statics (the theory of bodies in equilibrium) and dynamics (the theory of actual motions of all possible bodies, free and constrained). In this standard sense, mechanics contained *no* theory of matter. For an epitome, see Lagrange 1788.

[31] See Calinger 1969 and Leduc & Dumouchel 2015. Some have cast it as a debate between 'Wolffians' and 'Newtonians.' I reject these labels. The former group agreed just on simplicity as criterion for substance, and nothing else. The 'Newtonians' had little in common apart from antipathy to Wolff. Exegetes ascribe them a commitment to 'Newtonian science,' but that is an empty label. So, I shall refer to them simply as 'monadists' and 'anti-monadists.'

[32] Baumgarten's *non-extended* monads were impenetrable: "if we posit several monads to exist, then – because they are impenetrable – they will exist outside each other" (*extra se invicem*; see Baumgarten, *Metaphysica*, §399, 14: 109; and cf. Watkins 2006, for discussion). Kant was familiar with this tract, which he used in the classroom at length. The other figure was Euler, who in *Researches on the origin of forces* had argued that all (impressed) forces are episodic contact actions caused by impenetrability (of bodies in relative motion to each other, seeking to occupy the same place). See Euler 1752b and Gaukroger 1982.

then called them 'physical monads.'[33] Admittedly, not all German Rationalists turned dualist; some stayed true to monadic idealism. Still, both Wolffians and their Leibnizian dissenters agreed that simplicity is a nonnegotiable constraint on substance metaphysics. That is, no doctrine is acceptable unless it makes substance into a partless *monas*, or 'simple being.'[34]

These ambient facts entail a task, or problem, which Kant takes up officially in *Monads*. The problem is that geometry and metaphysics cannot be 'combined,' that is, used jointly to ground natural philosophy. Namely, each discipline entails an individual thesis that negates the other. Consider these inferential chains. [*geometry*] Space-divisibility entails that any finite bit of extension has finite proper parts. In turn, each part has its own extended parts; and so on, to no end. So, no extended simple or partless unity obtains in space. [*metaphysics*] Genuine substance is partless. There exist located bodies, and they are composites of material 'elements.' So, there are matter simples, or partless unities in space.

Evidently, these two conclusions are incompatible, which puts their entailing disciplines in conflict. Prima facie, then, combining metaphysics and geometry yields a conceptual nutcracker than crushes natural philosophy by denying it a coherent notion of body.

Substance

Kant's way out of this predicament is a type of material substance invulnerable to that nutcracker. To signal that it is simple but not mindlike, he calls it 'physical monad.' Precisely put, his monad is an object with three causal powers, which he calls 'forces.' They are, respectively, the force of inertia, of repulsion, and attraction. The latter two are actions at a distance. He posits that they obey power laws and speculates that repulsion is an inverse-cube force, and attraction is inverse-square.[35]

A physical monad has two 'spaces' associated with it. Namely, it exerts different causal powers over different-sized regions. The spaces are:

- place – a *point*-sized region where inertia resides and the two forces originate. He calls it the "place" taken up by the "mere positing" of a substance; that is, by just asserting it to exist, without regard to its causal activities (1: 483).

---

[33] See his *Cosmologia generalis*, Wolff 1731: § 137. For lucid analysis, see Hogan 2007 and Watkins 2006.

[34] In Wolff's 1730 *Philosophia prima, sive Ontologia* a full two thirds is taken up by his 'theory of simple being.' Kant regards these terms as exact synonyms: *simple substances, monads, elements of matter*, and *fundamental parts of body* (1: 477).

[35] *Monads*, 1: 480–1. In our terms, these forces are scalar potentials induced by a point-sized source. Both forces are irrotational and spheric-symmetric: Their gradient ∇ always points toward or away from the source, and the value of ∇ is the same at any two locations equidistant from the source.

- sphere of activity – a finite-sized, spherical volume. Its bounding surface S is the set of points where the monad's repulsive and attractive forces balance each other.[36] Anywhere below this surface there is net repulsion: Any other monad must expend momentum to reach below S, and when it comes to rest there, it will be scattered back. At the center of S, the repulsive force becomes infinite. Not by fiat, but because of the law of repulsive force.

I offer this distinction to elucidate Kant's thesis that "any monad not only *is* in space, but it also fills space," namely, a tiny volume.[37] So, *two* spaces are associated with a physical monad: the one that the monad 'is in' and the one that it 'fills.' In sum, a monad is in a space the size of a point, and it fills a space the size of a small sphere.

This conceptual innovation lets Kant solve the problem he uncovered. To help see it, I introduce a pair of operations on things with space properties:[38]

- s-divisibility; slicing – to conceive a mental plane intersecting a material volume. *Mutatis mutandis* for material surfaces or lines.
- b-divisibility; breaking – to conceive that adjoining parts (of a matter volume) have become separated by a net distance. Alternatively, to destroy some proper part of that volume, whether by physical causes or by divine action.

Their logical relations are as follows. 'Breaking' entails 'slicing': Any possible b-division conceptually requires an act of s-division. However, 'slicing' does *not* entail 'breaking.' Not every possible s-division can result in a b-division. This is shown by counterexamples; the best known and strongest was Absolute Space.[39] The physical monad is another. In effect, Kant exploits the conceptual asymmetry between 'slicing' and 'breaking' to show that we can have a substance that is not b-divisible.

To understand his solution, it is crucial to keep in mind the two associated spaces; in particular, that monadic 'place' is just the size of a *point*, and 'sphere

---

[36] In our terms, the sphere results from adding two vector fields, $\mathbf{r}(x)$ and $\mathbf{a}(x)$, where x is the distance to the center of S; $\mathbf{r}$ and $\mathbf{a}$ a point away from, and toward the center, respectively. To get the sphere of activity, impose the condition that $\mathbf{r}(x) + \mathbf{a}(x) > 0$.

[37] *Spatiolum*, 1: 480; translation slightly amended, my emphasis.

[38] An older exegesis relies on a similar distinction, viz. 'formal' and 'metaphysical' divisibility – cf. Holden (2004: 11–12). I suggest that mine is preferable to his. Mine is a univocal notion articulated within the single framework of relations between points. Holden's notion equivocates on 'division,' because his 'intellectual divisibility' is just another name for concept analysis, and results in relations between concepts, not space-parts. Thus, Holden's 'divisibility' is not a genus term with four species.

[39] The parts of Absolute Space (viz. absolute places) cannot be moved relative to each other: It is conceptually impossible, Newton had argued in *De gravitatione* (2014: 39). That makes Absolute Space immune to b-division. No entity can break it, not even God.

of activity' is a *finite* volume. Both are indivisible in just the right respects. (1) The place is indivisible in every relevant sense: It cannot be 'sliced,' 'broken,' or ruptured. Recall that 'slicing' requires mentally producing a *lesser*-dimensional geometric object inside the thing to be 'sliced' (i.e., a plane slices a volume, a line slices a plane, etc.). But a point is a *zero*-dimensional object. So, it is conceptually impossible to 'slice' it. Nor is it possible to 'break' it, as a point has no proper parts to separate or annihilate. Therefore, we cannot 'break' the resident *monad* at that place either. (2) The monad's sphere of activity is divisible, but in a safe sense: it can be 'sliced' but not 'broken.' That sphere is really just a spherical field of acceleration; thus neither it nor its parts are movable independently of their generating source, that is, the point-sized monad qua source of the repulsion field.[40] So, the monad's filled space is b-*indivisible*. These ideas seem the natural reading of his claim that

> Any line or surface dividing a tiny volume induces a part of space to exist outside the other, and vice versa. ... Now what exists on either side (of this dividing line) is not anything separable from its substance in such a way that, if we removed it from the substance, it would keep existing on its own. ... It is really an action exerted by one and the same substance. Thus, it is a relation – and so, finding a plurality in it does not amount to a substance being torn apart.
> So, in filling space, a monad exerts an action, viz. in a space determined on every side. Hence, we must grant that it fills this space by its sphere of activity. ... This filled space is the extent of an element's external presence. And so, dividing this space amounts to dividing the extensive magnitude of the presence of that substance. (1: 480–1)

Thereby Kant's physical monad avoids the threat of space-divisibility-cum-substantial-simplicity that he set out to avoid.

Body

As a corollary bonus, his solution yields an answer to a problem besetting monadologies (such as Wolff's) that had refused Leibniz's idealist way out of it. That problem was the *origin of body*.

Leibniz, Wolff, and their successors believed that matter is continuous. And Leibniz knew that the mathematical continuum (and any piece of finite

---

[40] Here is an illustration. Let P be a physical monad, and R some point inside its sphere of activity. Let R be identifiable by its distance from P and the strength of P's repulsive force at R. Suppose that, at time t_1, P and R are located at two points in space a and b, respectively. Now let P move until at time t_2 it arrives at space-point c. Then, *at that same time*, R will be at some space-point d that lies at the same distance from c as b was from a. This fact obtains throughout the time that P travels in space – really, at any instant during P's existence. Translated in Kant's words, this is just to say that a monad's sphere of activity cannot be broken apart, not separated from the monad itself.

extension) cannot be assembled from points. So, if monads are extensionless and pointlike, whereas a body is extended and continuous, then a body cannot result from aggregating monads. Leibniz solved this problem elegantly, by switching to thoroughgoing idealism about substance.[41] Wolff, whose 'physical monads' were not mindlike, had no coherent solution to this problem.

Kant found another solution, as unprecedented as it is ingenious. The matter theory in *Monads* entails that a body arises by physical composition, as follows. Any two or more physical monads can form an equilibrium configuration. Intuitively, that obtains when a monad sits on the bounding surface of another monad's sphere of activity (Figure 4, left). Namely, when A rests at a distance from B where B's attractive and repulsive forces balance each other. Let that distance be d. Whenever two or more physical monads come to be at d units away from each other, they will remain at relative rest. That is their equilibrium configuration. The configuration is fairly stable: When outside forces push or pull on any monad F in the configuration, F entrains the other monads in it, and they vibrate (relative to each other) around their positions of equilibrium.

In this picture, a body is any set of physical monads in an equilibrium configuration. In modern terms, it is a lattice of mass-points. That way of composing a body counts as physical because Kant-monads do that – they reach mutual equilibrium – by means of physical forces (of attraction and repulsion) that they carry *ab initio*.

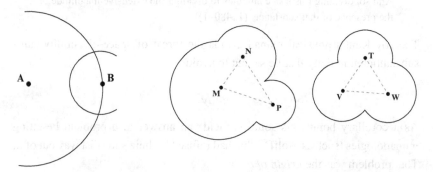

Figure 4 Bodies composed of monads. Left: B sits at the distance where A's repulsion and attraction add up to zero. Center and right: Monads M, N, P are endowed with respectively unequal forces (of attraction or repulsion), whereas V, T, and W's respective forces are of the same strength.

---

[41] That is, Leibniz endowed all substance with representational powers. In that doctrine, extended bodies count as *intentional* objects of monadic 'perception,' at least on some readings. The later Leibniz spoke in many voices on the origin of bodies; see Hartz 2007 for a review of his positions.

Finally, note an important fact. The young Kant *discarded* the Leibniz-Wolff tenet that bodies are continuous matter. Bodies assembled from Kant-monads are *discrete*: Between any two neighboring monads there is a small but finite distance of empty space – or at least it is empty of mass, though is it 'filled' with two acceleration fields of attraction and repulsion, to be sure. Still, at this stage in his thought, bodies just *appear* continuous. At the length-scales of human perception, a body's mass seems distributed continuously over the volume it takes up. But at microscopic scales and below, bodies are structured as lattices of mass-points.[42] This fact is worth signaling, because it separates the young Kant not just from his German predecessors, but also from his later views on matter, to which I now turn.

Matter Theory in the Critical Years

In richness and scope, the picture of matter in *Foundations* exceeds all early modern precedent, not just his youthful exercises in *Monads*. At the same time, Kant kept his exposition very compressed, and though he had occasions to expand on it later, he declined. That is regrettable, because obscurity pervades his book, and any chance to cast light on it would have helped his case with the reader.

A source of particular difficulty is the Table of Categories. From the Critique it reaches into his philosophy of physics, but it is hard to see what work it does there. Kant put it to several uses, sometimes as heuristic, sometimes as constraint on theorizing, and even as evidence for laws. I revisit this confounding aspect in Section III; for now, I examine his solutions to the early modern agenda in matter theory.

The Nature of Matter

Kant's transcendental program notwithstanding, a key part of his late picture comes from conceptual analysis. He seeks a list of *Teilbegriffe*, or parts that jointly make up the concept of matter. In a nutshell, he takes them to be three, as follows:

⟨matter⟩ $=^{def}$ mobile, impenetrable, and inert extension

Remarkably stable across his Critical years, this list is just the minimal account, as it were. Starting from it, some complex reasoning leads Kant to further

---

[42] To reiterate, this clean view is an artifice of exegesis. Kant's words in *Monads* allow us to extract it neatly from him – but they likewise suggest another view, incompatible with this one, and perhaps a *third* theory of matter, lurking behind his occasional confusions in the paper. A cogent, sharp dissection of his views there is Smith 2013.

determinations (of matter) co-extensive with the list; I summarize them at the end of the subsection. Now I discuss his concept-parts, introduced by single 'explications,' at the outset of his chapters.

Mobility

In the nature of matter, the first ingredient is mobility: "matter is the movable in space" (480). Two aspects about this notion deserve some discussion. First, mobility counts as a basic attribute for him. Namely, it is explanatorily fundamental relative to the other essential properties of matter: "[I]f anything should be an object of outer sense, its basic determination must be motion, for only through motion can that sense be affected."[43] Kant means his reductivism weakly, as just explanatory reduction: All other properties co-natural to matter are connected explanatorily to mobility, be it as causes of motion (e.g., the original forces of matter) or as its generic effects (e.g., being movent by transferring momentum).[44]

Second, in *Foundations* mobility is an equivocal notion: Kant in effect has two concepts of motion, and they are distinct. One is fit for single points of matter, the other works with extended bodies. The former concept is implicit and presupposed by his definition of speed as $C=S/T$.[45] This quantity implies that motion is change (over time) in the Cartesian coordinates of a free particle. His other concept is "change of outer relations to a given space" (482). But he gives no indication what those relations may be, if they are quantifiable, and how. So, we do not know if his second motion-concept can support a mathematized theory of matter in motion. This is a pity, because his picture of matter in *Dynamics* requires much stronger quantities of motion than the rudimentary kinematics he allowed himself in *Phoronomy*.[46]

In sum, the nature of matter is to be mobile, but in two senses. One is implicit and quantitative, the other is explicit but just verbal-qualitative.

---

[43] *Foundations*, 476. This claim has caused much exegesis and disagreement. A lucid account and defense of Kant's idea is McLear 2018.

[44] Contrast this view with strong programs (e.g., Descartes, Hobbes) for whom reducibility was ontological: All the (trans-kinematic) properties of matter *are* motions, nothing else. Each property supervenes on some specific, local pattern of matter in motion.

[45] His C is *celeritas*, the particle's speed at an instant. S is *spatium*, a finite rectilinear stretch the particle would cross in some time T if it kept moving at the speed C.

[46] For mater that is extended, continuous and deformable (as Kant has it) motion must be defined as any combination of translation, rigid rotation, and deformation over an instant. Each of them requires new, irreducible basic quantities. For instance, rigid rotation requires the mathematical concepts of Euler angles and the rotation matrix, and deformation requires notions like deformation gradient and some measure of strain. None of them can be had from Kant's formula $C=S/T$. For details and application to Kant's doctrine, see Stan 2017.

Impenetrability

Kant uses 'impenetrability' and 'space filling' synonymously, though he prefers the latter. What he really means by space-filling is that any body takes up a finite volume to the exclusion of any other body, at any given instant. Among the early moderns he is alone in trying to *explain* impenetrability.[47] That is, he rejects the view (then common) that no two bodies can collocate, because of a primitive, analytic-conceptual property constitutive of body, namely, their impenetrability. To the contrary, he argues, impenetrability is universal but *derivative:* Failure of collocation is an effect induced by a material property explanatorily upstream from it. The property is a force of repulsion: "Matter fills its space through repulsive force" (499). The force is causally responsible for matter 'filling space,' namely, taking up a volume and resisting *its* penetration; it does so by way of repelling any other body seeking to enter that filled volume.

Since failure of collocation obtains universally, and because repulsion is responsible for its obtaining, it follows that matter is 'originally' endowed with a force to repel other matter bits universally: "matter is impenetrable, namely, through its original expansive force." He counts this result as a theorem (503).

Further, if exerting repulsive force is universal to matter, so is having a force of attraction, he claims: "Repulsive force belongs to the essence of matter just as much as attractive force; neither one can be left out from the concept of matter" (511). He thinks attraction is co-essential to matter because he infers it *from* the fact of repulsion being essential – via his Balance Argument, an inference he had devised in his youth.

Inertia

Another property Kant ascribes to matter is being inert. In the century after Huygens and Newton, natural philosophers had turned inertia into a generous term denoting three distinct patterns of behavior, as follows. No single body accelerates itself: All changes to its velocity are due to outside agencies. Conservation of linear motion: absent exogenous actions, a body in translation will stay in that state. Resistance to force: Bodies respond to force differentially – a given force will accelerate two different bodies by different

---

[47] In an unpublished fragment, Leibniz had said body takes up a volume impenetrably not in virtue of a metaphysical attribute (Cartesian extension) but because of a "passive force" spreading outward over that volume (1989: 251). But Leibniz did not *argue* for it, whereas Kant did so for his claim. And, understood as failure of collocation, impenetrability also counts as an effect in Boscovich's doctrine: Getting two 'physical points' to overlap never happens, because the required force is infinite. However, this is just an unstated corollary of his doctrine; Boscovich does not explain it, nor does he discuss its philosophical import.

amounts.[48] Kant's notion of inertia keeps the first two strands, though not the third (see below).

Take the fact of null self-acceleration first; it is his second law of mechanics: "All change in matter has an external cause" (543). He considers it a metaphysical principle, and purports to derive it by deductive argument from generic facts about the ontology of body. His key fact is that "matter has no purely internal determinations nor grounds of determination." So, he concludes, no piece of matter can cause itself to change its state of motion. From this result he infers bluntly, as if it were an easy corollary, the second fact: A body "persists in its state of rest or of motion in the same direction at the same speed" if left to itself.[49]

More alarmingly, *Foundations* kept no trace of his earlier thought – a real insight – that inertia is primarily *resistance* to exogenous action. That creates a problem for his metaphysics of matter.

Body

His ideas above yield a concept of body, understood as "a matter within determinate boundaries, hence one that has a shape" (525). Put modernly, a Kant-body is a finite volume K of matter bounded by a determinate surface S. K has all the properties that *Foundations* assigns to matter in general: It is mobile, impenetrable, inert, it carries momentum, and has objective states of motion. He says little about what makes shape S determinate. Presumably, he would think it is the surface such that, at every point on it, the body's overall force of repulsion balances its net attraction.[50]

For more light on his view, I offer a contrastive account between his early and Critical notions of body, seen from two angles. One is mass distribution. The young Kant thought that bodies were discrete, but later he changed his mind, and argued that bodies really are continuous.[51] Another one is part–whole

---

[48] These concepts are explained (and contextualized relative to eighteenth-century doctrines, not just Kant's) in Brading & Stan 2023, who call it the 'problem of elusive mass.'

[49] *Foundations*, 543. Other exegetes have noted that Kant shows no interest in proving the "positive part" of the law of inertia, viz. the continuance of rest or uniform translation; see Friedman (2013: 338) and Watkins (2019: 132).

[50] This answer is plausible as a reading of Kant, but it would not suffice to account for S. In general, other, more specific factors are needed to explain why S is *that* determinate surface, rather than some other shape (that the body K could have and remain compatible with the general principles of mechanics). For example, in fluids S is partly determined by the body-*external* force that walls (containing the fluid) exert on it. In solids, by the body-internal forces of *cohesion*, which – even by Kant's reckoning – is a force different from his 'original attraction.'

[51] We can put the point exactly. *Monads* implies that, at every point in a body K, its associated value of mass is either zero of a finite quantity. *Foundations* presupposes that the value at a point is neither zero nor finite; it is infinitesimal. Recall, the net mass of a continuous body is the integral of values at every point in it; see formula (2), and also Appendix B at the end of this Element.

relations. Over three decades, he came to rethink his view of them entirely. In *Monads*, the parts are prior to the whole, explanatorily and ontologically. They explain why the body that they make up has the parameters that it has: because its quantities are just arithmetic sums of the determinate parameters that its component monads have. And they subsist – individually, down to single monads – before and after the contingent body that they make up has come in and gone out of existence. Speaking traditionally, physical monads are actual parts of bodies. In *Foundations*, however, bodies have just potential parts; and every part depends on its body in two ways. Explanatorily, parameter-values associated with any part obtain as 'limitations' of whole-body parameters.[52] Ontologically, any part depends (for its becoming actual) on acts of division, physical or just mental, done on the body.

Inertia, Quantity Concepts, and Mass

While early modern science moved far beyond the Scholastic and Renaissance pictures of matter that preceded it, none of its innovations made such a radical break with the past as the idea that matter bears a universal, quantitative property we call mass. Newton grasped that fact for the first time, and even he had to struggle with it – first to see it at all, then to see it clearly.

The fact is, inertial mass is a subtle and elusive concept – it remains so to our day – and, because of that, the early moderns tended to conflate into one picture two distinct ideas:[53]

- Mass measures a body's response to force. Call this 'inertial mass.'
- Mass measures a body's physical agency. Call this 'material mass,' or 'quantity of matter.'

Now for some elucidation. For the first idea, begin with a salient fact: The more mass a thing has, the less it can be moved, or displaced from its position. Suppose two bodies at rest in empty space, and let their respective masses be k and l, with k greater than l; let two equal forces of strength f act on them simultaneously during some time t. Mass k being greater than l is the reason why k will have moved a shorter distance than l, at the end of the time t. That is, other

---

[52] In mathematized treatments of continuous matter, one starts with a finite part P inside the body, sometimes called an 'Euler Cut,' or 'control volume.' Values for mass- and force-density associated with P are given by a series (of decreasing volumes) converging onto P. In situations that require great rigor (e.g., deriving the equations of motion for the body), we let P shrink to size zero – to a volume element dV, the smallest part in a continuous body – and we infer to the value of mass and force acting on dV.

[53] For explanations of Newton's hard-won insight into inertial mass (which did not occur until 1685 at the earliest) see Biener & Smeenk 2012, Fox 2016, and Smith 2019. For a discussion of the various mass-concepts peddled in the period from Newton to Kant, see Brading & Stan 2023.

things being equal, if a body has more k, it moves less than the one having l. This is the content behind the idea that, in a body, mass is the *measure of resistance to acceleration* by an applied force.

To elucidate the idea of material mass, another salient fact. Beside resisting force, mass is the key ingredient in certain fundamental behaviors. The more mass a body has, the more it can displace another object in its path. The more mass it has, the more it fills space – by making its volume more densely packed with matter. And, the more mass it has, the stronger it attracts other bodies passing nearby. In careful terms, these behaviors mean that mass is a co-measure of momentum (alongside velocity), a co-measure of density (alongside volume), and also a co-measure of gravitational attraction (alongside passive gravitational charge).[54] Hence, mass is a *measure of physical agency*.

In sum, regarded as a quantity concept, mass is the single measure of a twofold attribute. Inertial mass measures a body's resistance to impressed forces; material mass measures its amount of agency qua physical object: its 'quantity of matter.'

With my clarification as a backdrop, we can see that Kant over the years oscillated between the two mass-concepts above. In his youth he endowed matter with mass qua inertial resistance. In *Monads*, every point-sized ultimate bit of matter carries two charges, attractive and repulsive, and also a third property:

> A body's force of inertia is the sum of the inertia forces of all the elements making up that body. . . . Given any element, others can likewise be given whose force of inertia can be twice or three times greater. . . . So, two bodies of equal volume may have very different *masses*, as their respective elements are endowed with greater or smaller forces of inertia. For, in bodies, mass is just the *quantity of their force of inertia* whereby they either *resist motion* or are able to *impel another* body, at some given speed (1: 485–6, my emphasis).[55]

Treating 'mass' and 'inertia' as synonymous is evidence that young Kant understood mass in the canonical sense (of Newton and modern theory), that is, as the measure of resistance to applied force.

---

[54] Mass is just the measure of the gravitational charge (active, not passive) that is the source of the attractive field (or gravitational potential) induced by a mass in the space around itself. Exactly how strong that field is at a point in space depends, in addition, on the distance from it to the field source.

[55] To say that inertia is a force, as Kant does, had become obsolete by 1756, when he wrote *Monads*, even though Newton too had called it *vis inertiae*. In particular, throughout the 1740s Euler had censured talk of inertia being a force. Put simply, Euler's lesson was that forces are *directed* magnitudes, whereas inertia is a scalar, directionless; and that forces cause *changes* of state, whereas inertia conserves states (of linear motion). So, inertia is not a force. See, inter alia, his 1746 paper *De la force de percussion et de sa veritable mesure*. Kant appears unfamiliar with Euler's lessons, perhaps because he wrote in French then, which Kant seemingly could not read.

However, this seems to have changed by the 1770s; *Foundations* lacks any reference to inertial mass. Instead, now another concept looms large, namely, 'quantity of matter.' Kant treats it as a genus concept with two species, 'dynamical' and 'mechanical' quantity of matter. I shorten them respectively as DQ and MQ, for convenience.

Dynamical quantity is a parameter used for explanatory work in Dynamics, the theory that accounts for matter being impenetrable: No two pieces of matter numerically distinct are collocated in the same volume. Kant makes this fact into a kinematic effect – of a 'dynamical' force of repulsion: Matter is impenetrable because it repels any object trying to occupy the volume that it (the matter) takes up.[56] This repulsive force is a compound quantity; DQ is a component quantity that co-determines the strength of the repulsion at any point below the body's surface (the other co-determining magnitude is some function of distance). At least that is how Kant speaks – as if 'quantity of repulsive force' and DQ are the same thing: "[I]f we must represent a greater or a smaller space as completely filled with the same quantity of matter, i.e., with one and the same amount [*Quantum*] of repulsive force ... The original [force of] attraction is proportional to the quantity of matter." (506, 518)

Now consider MQ, the mechanical species of his genus-concept. He defines it in the discipline that requires it, namely, in mechanics qua theory of momentum exchanges. In *that* context, Kant lets 'quantity of matter' be the measure of two cognate attributes of body: counting as a material substance and being movent.[57]

> The quantity of matter is the aggregate of movables [contained] in a given volume. If we regard its parts (while they move) as acting together – by being movent – the aggregate is called the *mass*. And so we say "a matter acts in mass" when its parts move jointly and exert their outward-movent force *together*. ... The quantity of motion, estimated as in mechanics, is the product of quantity of moved matter and its common velocity. ...
>
> Thus we can see how quantity of substance must be estimated just mechanically, or via the quantity of its own motion – not dynamically, i.e., not from the amount of original moving forces. (537, 541; original emphasis)

---

[56] In modern terms, if a piece of matter A moves to enter a volume currently occupied by another piece, B, then it will have to *deform* B, upon contact. For Kant, deforming a body's bounding surface (by bending it inward) will cause repulsive forces to build up on the deformed surface. These forces will repel A – out of the region V, previously occupied by B in its undeformed state – and so B will revert to occupying B, just as it did before A entered its space by penetrating it. An excellent explanation of Kant's mode of thinking there is Smith 2013.

[57] For the latter attribute, Kant used *bewegend*, best translated as 'movent,' a vintage term for the ability to displace a thing and thereby set it in motion.

In sum, mechanical quantity of matter, MQ, generally denotes the *size of agency* that a body qua determinate volume of matter exerts in processes of momentum transfer.

But note what is missing from Kant's picture above: that matter *resists* applied forces – and any attempt at displacement (by a movent, or carrier of momentum). That is the crucial insight behind the correct notion of inertia. Different bodies resist a given force to different extents. Mass, qua measure of inertia, expresses the amount to which specific bodies resist the action of external forces.

Among practitioners of exact science, this fact was incontrovertible by 1786; decades before then Euler had made it canonical. And yet, Kant in the Critical decade never took it up philosophically. Rather, his interest seems to lie elsewhere: in redefining inertia – by explaining it with a polemical intent, to set straight what he perceives as misunderstandings. This corrective endeavor seems to have held his attention for some decades; already in the 1770s he pursued it in the classroom; and then in *Foundations*, the locus of his official, considered views on inertia, mass, and their relation:

> The inertia of matter is, and denotes, nothing but its lifelessness, qua matter in itself. ... Thus, all matter as matter is *lifeless*. The law of inertia says just that, nothing more. ... The denial of this law, and thus the death of all natural philosophy, would be the doctrine of *hylozoism*. From the above concept (of inertia qua mere *lifelessness*) falls out directly that inertia does not denote any *positive striving* by matter to preserve its state. (544)[58]

These corrective moves are understandable if we enlarge the context.[59] Still, it remains a fact that he became distracted by minor polemics, to the detriment of completeness of foundations. That is, no matter what else one might wish inertia to denote, one must not lose sight of what inertia *is*, according to the exact science of nature: resistance to force. Kant knew this crucial fact in his youth, but then allowed himself to forget it. *Foundations* shows no trace of his earlier, true thought that mass measures inertia and that inertia is primarily resistance to

---

[58] In our terms: For any piece of matter the self-acceleration is zero. Kant equates that with lifelessness. Hence, the kinematico-dynamical content of his *leblos* is that the self-force and the self-acceleration on a body are always null. Nothing about his term 'lifeless' entails that matter *resists* forces exerted from outside that piece of matter.

[59] Kant here castigates two groups. One is the Wolffians, who posited that matter has a 'force of inertia' whereby they resist motion, primarily in collision. (For details, see Stan 2013.) Rather uncharitably, Kant construes it as a power to *do* something. The other is Maupertuis, who had conjectured *material* particles, or 'elements,' that set themselves in motion, viz. accelerate from within, animated by analogues of desire; cf. his *Système de la nature*, first published in Latin (1751), which Kant read. He may well have a point against both groups, but he seems needlessly polemic. By the time of *Foundations*, Wolff and Maupertuis had been long dead, and no one called it *vis inertiae* any longer; nor did self-accelerating 'elements' survive Maupertuis.

external force. In fact, now he rails against conceiving of inertia as an agency of any kind, even a resistive one: "The inertia of matter, viz. the bare impotence to move itself, is not the cause of *any* resistance" (551; my emphasis). His change of heart from *Monads* is strange, little motivated, and costly. It was this absence (of the right notion of inertia) that led me to say that ultimately he lacks a full concept of mass.

My point is stronger than that; I do not mean just the contingent fact that Kant by 1786 seems to have forgotten the true meaning of mass, which he once knew. I mean to raise the worry that we do not know if the proper meaning *can* be recovered from his basis in *Foundations* and then retrofitted to his theoretical architecture in the book. Where would it go – where in his foundations would it fit, and how?

This problem is far from easy. Kant's grounding enterprise proceeds under self-imposed but stringent conditions that carry over from the Critique: The Analytic of Concepts constrains what he may build into the metaphysics of *Foundations*. More precisely put, Kant pursues a project in constitution theory: He starts with category-structures proven in the Analytic, and from them he aims to obtain the essence of bodyhood, namely, the full list of *Teilbegriffe* making up our concept of body. In *Foundations*, that innovative approach succeeds too well, apparently: It leaves no room, architectonic or explanatory, for inertial mass, that is, the concept of mass qua measure of resistance to force. Architectonically, Kant's official list of 'concept parts' seems complete, and inertial mass is not on it; to be sure, 'mechanical quantity of matter' does make it onto his list, but that is *not* inertial mass. Explanatorily, inertial mass measures a *resistive* property of matter, but Kant's categories allow only *activity* features (of corporeal substance) among the conceptual inventory of his book. Perhaps sensing that fact, Kant had to keep an *incomplete* concept of inertia (being unable to retain the full concept of it), in that he singled out for analysis just the aspects that make it consilient with substantial *agency*, broadly speaking. To be precise, in placing inertia under the categories of relation, he had to truncate it into a concept denoting just an activity-supporting feature of matter, with no trace of matter's resistive roles. In his account, inertia entails just that a body's accelerating *itself* always equals zero; and that responsibility for causal action on a body (with acceleration as the generic effect) is traceable to some body other than itself:

> Matter ... undergoes no other changes except through motion. In regard to them – qua change from one motion to another, from motion to rest, or vice versa – there must be a cause (by the principles of metaphysics). Now this cause cannot be internal, for matter has no purely internal determinations or grounds thereof. So, any change of a matter is grounded in outer causes. (543)

Again, this concept of inertia is incomplete: It leaves out that inert matter *resists* forces; and that mass quantifies that outward-directed resistance.

Now I put my point in historical terms. Natural philosophers before Kant knew that inertia discloses to us that all matter *resists agency* or is resistive (to changes of state) just as much as it might otherwise be active. Inertial mass is just the numeric face of this resistive behavior. Because of this insight – that matter resists too, besides acting – mass is a Janus-faced concept: It measures both agency and resistance. Kant knew this fact in his youth, but his mature systematic commitments seem to have kept him from doing it full explanatory justice. He could only afford to account for its activity-denoting half, namely, the property whereby matter behaves as a momentum-carrier. That is the insight behind his term, 'mechanical quantity of matter,' partial though it is.

To sum up, the later Kant's understanding of mass is non-standard in two respects: He no longer explicates it as the measure of inertia; and he does not explicate inertia as resistance to acceleration.

Quantification

Another vantage point reveals that Kant's mature doctrine of matter lacks a full notion of inertial mass. That vantage point is quantification, or his account of how we mathematize the empirical features of body conveyed by the notion 'quantity of matter.'[60] Explaining how science mathematizes matter is really a dual task. It required an early modern philosopher to justify two things, namely:

1. The matter making up any one body has a magnitude structure.
2. 'Quantity of matter' has a stable, universal empirical measure.

I explicate them below, then I examine Kant's account of them critically, to see how sound it is; let Q stand for his 'quantity of matter.'

Additivity

Q has a quantity structure if it is an *additive* property: For any aggregate of matter-parts, its Q is the arithmetic sum of the Q values associated with each of its parts.[61]

---

[60] It is Friedman's merit to have drawn attention to this crucial yet much neglected part of Kant's natural philosophy, and to have spelled out its details with much care. See, in particular, Friedman 2012 and his monumental 2013.

[61] The 'arithmetic' part is not optional. Some writers use the phrase 'mereological sum.' I do not know what that is, unless it is just another name for set-theoretic union. I for one mean 'sum' here in the arithmetic sense, viz. as the output of iterating the operator '+,' or of performing mentally the operation it denotes.

Kant's Natural Philosophy

At this juncture, his philosophy of mathematics becomes relevant. To vindicate condition (1), he must show that addition for Q is constructable a priori, that is, we can represent in pure intuition the operation of adding Qs into a Q-sum. That is because in *Foundations* he gave himself the task of showing that another physical property (namely, velocity) counts as a quantity because it is 'composable' in intuition, or additive: "To construct concepts, it is required ... that the condition of their constructing must not be a concept that cannot be at all given a priori in intuition. This much we must establish wholly a priori and intuitively on behalf of applied mathematics. ... The question [in Phoronomy] is how the concept of velocity is *constructed* as a magnitude." But, Q is likewise a property of matter that needs mathematizing. So, it too must be shown to be composable in pure intuition.[62]

Asserting Q of matter-bits depends in part on the architecture of matter. Namely, ascribing determinate Q-values to parts of matter – then making claims about their sum – depends on one's matter theory: How matter at fundamental levels is *distributed in space* constrains the *mathematical form* of Q-statements about matter. In more intuitive terms, a summation claim about mass points differs (in regard to mathematical structure) from a summation claim about matter qua physical continuum. Consider how we express mathematically that a body's Q is the sum of the Q-magnitudes associated with its parts. Let K and G be two bodies, and K be made of j discrete point-particles, while G is physically continuous; and let q_i be the quantity of matter associated with each particle in K, whereas **q** denotes the density of quantity-of-matter for each element of volume in the continuous body G. Here is how we say that K's quantity Q is the finite sum of its discrete parts:

$$Q_K = \sum_j q_j \qquad (1).$$

And for G, a continuous body that takes up a volume V in space:

$$Q_G = \int_V \mathbf{q}\, dV \qquad (2).$$

Put in our terms, one is a Riemann sum over a finite set, the other is a volume integral, or infinite sum of infinitely small elements. Kant in 1786 thinks that matter is continuous – so, representing a body's quantity of matter involves a Type-2 expression.

Now I must raise a worry: What is **q**? We know the answer – it is the mass density (at a point), namely, the ratio of *inertial* mass over the volume it occupies.

---

[62] Really, this condition is just a local corollary (for the case of quantity of matter) of Kant's general view that summation-statements are synthetic a priori, not analytic. Recall his famous thesis that '7 + 5 = 12' is true in virtue of a constructed intuition, not conceptual-containment facts.

But what would *he* say it denotes? It turns out that Kant gave the wrong answer, in effect denying himself the chance of giving the correct one. He says:

> Note: the quantity of matter is the quantity of substance in a movable thing. So, it is *not the size of some quality* of it. ... Here, the amount of substance denotes nothing but the *mere sum of the movable* making up that thing. For, only this sum of the movable can make a difference in quantity of motion (if the speed is given). (540 f, my emphasis)

For transparency, I put his point in modern terms. Kant above claims that, in an extended body, its quantity of substance is the volume-integral of the *velocity*, because he thinks that two points in a continuous body differ at most in their degrees of speed, and *nothing* else. This makes clear how he went astray: In reality, points in a physical continuum can differ from each other in respect of their velocities *and also* in the values of inertial-mass density at those points. That is the insight behind formula (2). It is that, in an extended body, its *total* mass is the sum of the *inertial*-mass values at every point in the body. These values can *vary* from point to point, even for a body in pure translation (i.e., whose points all have the same velocity); and they differ in *kind* from the velocity-values that obtain at every point in a moved body. Thus, a look at how he explains quantifying matter confirms my verdict above that *Foundations* lacks a proper concept of mass.

The right conception is that mass is an exact synonym of inertia: Mass is the numeric aspect of a body's being inert by resisting linear acceleration. Mass is the quantity of linear inertia at a point.[63] But, this synonymy seems absent from *Foundations*. Kant there uses 'mass' for the *output of summing* over corporeal parts (541). Let *B* be an extended body, and grant Kant his notion of an 'independently movable' part: Any part of *B* that (by means of applied forces) we could cause to move separately from *B*; for instance, by detaching it from *B*. Tacitly, he means the *least* such part.[64] Then by 'mass' Kant in *Foundations* means the sum, or total amount, of the independently movable parts in a body. But that is not what classical physics means by mass. Hence, Kant mass and inertial mass are distinct concepts. His term seems quite close to the meaning of mass in the phrase 'mass noun.' In his usage, mass is a feature of the whole, not a quantitative property (the degree of resistance) of every part in it. And, thereby he forgot to explain *what* gets added, when we compute the mass of an aggregate: What is the intensive magnitude (at every point) that we integrate over, so as infer to the mass of the whole body?

---

[63] Resisting rotation is measured by a different property, viz. moment of inertia. Mass measures just how hard it is to accelerate bodies in a straight line, not in a curve.

[64] If we regard *B* as a discrete aggregate, then an independently movable part is any particle that make up *B*. If we consider it continuous, then those parts are the elements d*V* making up the volume of *B*.

Lastly, note that Kant would not incur this problem, had he kept his old theory from *Monads*. In his youth he had a ready answer to our query about the meaning of q_j above. He would have said that q_j measures the 'force of inertia' associated with a single physical monad j.

Measure

Condition (2) requires some backdrop.[65] Just like 'force,' 'temperature,' and 'charge,' 'mass' is a theoretical term: It denotes a property not given in perception. With such properties, we must *infer* to their presence and size from other properties that *are* given to the senses. In particular, making size claims about theoretical properties requires us to rely – indispensably, as *evidence* for such claims – on facts about the behavior of perceptible counterparts for them: Some sensible property that tracks changes in the theoretical one at issue. The name for this generic approach is 'measuring by proxy.' Through it, we use measurements of the sensible property qua epistemic proxies for size claims about the perceptually unavailable theoretical property.

For this approach to be sound, the theoretical term at issue must have *robust* proxies. Specifically, since mass is a non-perceptual feature of body, we must secure some empirical property that meets two criteria. (i) The property is universally accessible, namely, it allows us to measure its value for any body, no matter how big or how far. (ii) The empirical property must vary linearly with the theoretical property for which it stands as a proxy.

In this regard, mass is a happy case, for it has a proxy both robust and eminently perceptible by Kantian criteria. That proxy is a species of *space-quantity*. More exactly, it is acceleration, namely, change of space-distance with respect to time, twice. Acceleration is special, because its aptness qua measurement-proxy for mass is guaranteed nomically – by Newton's laws of motion. In particular, the Second Law in conjunction with the law of universal gravitation entails that for any body K, its mass correlates with the acceleration it causes on any *other* body G; and also with its *own* acceleration, whenever K interacts with any part of the world. That is,

$$(m_K \approx \mathbf{a}_G) \tag{3},$$

$$m_K \approx \mathbf{a}_K \tag{4}.$$

---

[65] The points that follow owe much to deeply stimulating discussions with Katherine Brading, and the late George E. Smith; I thank them gratefully.

Here I must clarify an aspect. Recall my point that, to be a suitable proxy measure for mass, an empirical property must be *universal*.[66] Acceleration meets that criterion, yet not by itself and unconditionally, but because of a force: There is one (and just one) causal power that induces accelerations fit to stand in as proxy measures of masses. That power is gravity. It is a universal force: It reaches wherever matter may exist. And, it is direct: It needs no intermediary to cause the proxy-accelerations that correlate with Q. These features of gravity secure condition (2) for Q to count as a legitimate quantification of matter, with empirical import – because it is the Law of Universal Gravity that underwrites the nomic correlations (3) and (4) above. In a nutshell, Kant takes his Q notion, connects it with static weight (namely, the corporeal property that on Earth we measure by weighing an object), and then extends the concept of terrestrial weight

> into a *universally applicable measure of mass valid for all bodies* in the universe, independently of their relation to the surface of the earth. Kant incorporates these key properties of Newtonian universal gravitation into his metaphysical foundation for natural science, by taking them to be *constitutive* of the empirical concept of matter that he is in the process of articulating. (Friedman 2012: 499; my emphasis)

I explain these matters in Appendix A; see also Friedman 2013.

Assessment

Friedman's construal (of Kant showing Q to have an apt empirical measure) is compelling, inspired, and without precedent. But if we inspect it closely, we discover that it rests on three key premises, two of them left tacit. These premises are: Newton's Second and Third Law; a statement nowadays called the Equivalence Principle; and the Law of Universal Gravity. I explain them below, and their challenge for Kant.

The Third Law is needed to guarantee that we can measure a body's 'quantity of matter' Q from *its own* acceleration.[67] But that law needs Newton's *Second* Law to give it meaning; without it, the Third Law is an empty statement – it lacks empirical content in terms of motion. Friedman's account needs Kant to rely on the Second Law twice. First, the law ensures that Q, the quantity of matter in a body K, is proportional to **b**, the acceleration that K induces (by its 'dynamical' force of attraction) in some *other* body, G. Second, to then infer that **b** is proportional to **a**, the acceleration that K in turn suffers from G acting on it reciprocally, as the Third Law dictates.

---

[66] That is because *mass* is universal, being an essential property of body.
[67] Again, see Appendix A for details.

But this raises some worries. The Second Law is entirely absent from Kant's metaphysical foundations. Not only does he not state it, but it is doubtful that he *could* have incorporated it. Consider its content:

$$\mathbf{f}_{impressed} = m \cdot \mathbf{a}$$

The law really says that a force's effect is proportional to m, the *inertial* mass of the body on which it acts. But again, Kant does not *have* a notion of inertial mass in his Critical metaphysics of nature. *A fortiori*, even less room does he have for a principle that depends on inertial mass for its very meaning, namely, the Second Law.[68]

Friedman's reading must rely on another key assumption. It is the Equivalence Principle: A body's inertial mass is equal to its 'heaviness,' or weight. That principle is needed to justify why we measure mass reliably by relying on gravity. Specifically, using gravity (e.g., by weighing a body) discloses how much 'heaviness' a body has: its weight, or "endeavor to move in the direction of greater gravity" around it (518). But weight (qua response to gravity) and inertial mass are distinct properties – conceptually and physically. And so, we need a *principled* justification that weight tracks mass, namely, that every act of accurately measuring a body's weight informs reliably us what the body's *inertial* mass is. That justification is called the Weak Equivalence Principle.[69] It says that, for any single body, its (Kantian) weight and its inertial mass are equal: Their ratio is 1:1. However, the Equivalence Principle is an *empirical* fact, not an a priori thesis. Newton had confirmed it by experiment, and in the 1700s no one had any purely philosophical warrant for it. Therefore, as we assess Kant's philosophical explanation of how we quantify matter, we must not lose sight of the empirical assumptions on which he relies.

The third key assumption is that gravity is universal, and its quantitative strength is as given by Newton in *Principia*.[70] Kant believes it beyond doubt, as Friedman has shown amply. Still, we may ask about the grounds for his confidence. There are two avenues. Kant could have accepted the Law of Universal Gravity based on Newton's evidence for it. Now the Briton's warrant was a long *inductive* argument, relying on orbital parameters inferred from decades of empirical data. That sort of evidence makes Newton's law of gravity

---

[68] I used to think that we can find a way to credit Kant with an implicit Second Law, extractable from the rest of his overt foundations. Having considered the matter carefully, I no longer think the law can be retrofitted to his foundations. *Mea culpa*. Eric Watkins seems to have reached the same conclusion (2019: 142–5).

[69] I explain these matters in Appendix B. See also Fox 2016, which explains lucidly how Newton discovered the Equivalence Principle in 1685.

[70] Namely, if r is the relative distance of two bodies, and m_1, m_2 are their masses, then they exert on each other a force proportional to $(m_1 \cdot m_2)/r^2$.

count as a posteriori knowledge; then we might wonder why Kant thinks that it belongs in the *metaphysics* of body. And it makes his case (that matter is quantifiable) ultimately contingent, not a priori certain, because it depends crucially on a contingent fact, namely, the kinematic effects of gravity in our solar system (they were Newton's evidence for his law).

Alternatively, suppose Kant relied not on Newton's own evidence but on stronger facts. Namely, on *identifying* gravity with his 'original attraction,' a metaphysical force for which he claims a priori warrant.[71] He suggests as much himself: "The effect of universal attraction – which matter exerts on any other matter, directly and at any distance – we call *gravity*. The endeavor to move in the direction of greater gravity is *weight*" (518). Clearly, identifying the two forces would obviate the worries I raised above. But, what justifies his thinking that they *are* identical – that gravity and 'original attraction' are the same force-species? What is the evidence for that? Not only is it a mystery, but, to further confound the reader, Kant in the next breath censures the thought that Newtonian gravity may rest on a priori warrant, which original attraction does: "We must not venture any law of force, attractive or repulsive, based on a priori conjectures. In fact, we must infer everything from *data of experience*. Even the universal attraction (as the cause of gravity), as well as its governing law" (534; my emphasis). What to make of these conflicting statements is for future exegesis.

The upshot of my discussion is that Kant's philosophical account of quantification – the application of mathematics to material bodies – requires some concepts that he lacks, for example, inertial mass; and some premises that are empirical, hence extraneous to metaphysics. More work is needed for us to discern exactly just how much quantification can be vindicated from his available, official resources.

In sum, a constant of Kant's long grappling with the constitution of matter was his rejection of extension-first doctrines. By that I mean the family of early modern views (by Descartes, Malebranche, d'Alembert, Euler, and Lambert) for whom extension was explanatorily basic, and force – if they admitted it – was an episodic action that occurs when impenetrable extendeds make contact. Kant was a force-first theorist. Against the neo-Cartesians, he proposed a picture in which corporeal extension is derivative: It obtains from force, namely, from the mutual balancing of two forces (attraction and repulsion)

---

[71] That a priori warrant comes from his Balance Argument. It starts with two premises: We have experience of matter in stable configurations; and 'original repulsion' is essential to it. From them Kant purports to infer that an 'original attractive force' is co-essential to matter. For lucid analysis, see Smith 2013.

that matter has 'originally' and exerts at all times. That matter has these two forces indispensably is the *Leitfaden* running through his natural philosophy.

Look underneath it, however, and you will see very significant changes. Based on my glosses, three stand out. First, in the 1750s Kant had not integrated explanatorily his matter theory (from *Monads*) and his dynamics of interaction (from *Motion*). By 1786, he had found a way to bring them together, though obscurely.[72] Second, his views on the microstructure of matter go through a seismic shift. On the most coherent and charitable construal, *Monads* is a theory of discrete mass-points; they are the actual parts of bodies.[73] In contrast, *Foundations* argues that matter is a physical continuum, and so all corporeal parts are potential, down to infinitesimal volume elements. Third, and most innovatively, the mature Kant became sensitive to the general problem of quantification in natural philosophy. In the Critical decade, we see him absorbed in explaining how physical theory associates quantity-concepts with pictures of matter. That project is a daunting task for any philosopher, including him. To the modern exegete, his work on quantifying matter reveals deep tension between his philosophy of mathematics and his ontology of body.[74] Commendably, Kant did not shirk from these hard problems. In the end, then, his metaphysics of matter made visible progress, though at great cost.

Epistemology

Difficult as they are, the intricacies of Kant's metaphysics pale next to the challenge of explaining the epistemology behind his views. It is the "hardest nut to crack," as Parsons put it, and a broader enigma that clouds rationalist foundations of early modern science.[75] Here I tackle the problem of how one might *know* the things that Kant has claimed so far. My heuristic is the dual question: What counts as *sources of evidence* for his views, and what *patterns of inference* take him from evidence to his claims?

To manage expectations, I start on a sobering note: Little about Kant's epistemology of applied metaphysics looks settled beyond exegetic dispute; many aspects are really items in a research agenda for the future. My study

---

[72] "The communication of motion [in impact] occurs only through the kind of moving forces that inhere in a matter at rest," namely, the 'dynamical' force of repulsion (551). That is all he offers, though. What is needed is a descriptive explanation – of how repulsive force (which acts on the *surface* of colliding bodies) ends up decelerating the *center* of mass (whose behavior Kant's doctrine tries to explain), which lies away from that surface, deep in the impacted body.

[73] I must remind the reader that *Monads* does not present a clean, single view of matter; cf. Smith 2013, who first discovered that fact.

[74] In particular, his theory of matter qua physical continuum requires a much stronger mathematical framework than he allowed himself. Continuous matter requires partial differential equations to handle; for explanations, see Smith 2013 and Stan 2017.

[75] See Parsons 2012, among the first to grapple with the epistemology of *Foundations*.

below amounts largely to unearthing problems, describing them clearly, and mapping their relations. The reader is invited to take them on.

Purity

I begin with an elucidation. Kant has a phrase, 'pure natural science,' that is as important to him as it is opaque. The term 'pure' is notoriously equivocal in his doctrine – he applies it both to sub-propositional representations and also to knowledge items. Thus, Kantian purity could be semantic or epistemological. So, claiming that there is a pure science of nature has two construals:

- s-pure science – knowledge that incorporates non-empirical concepts. Their semantic content is not gained by acquaintance, abstraction from perceptions, idealization from material setups, or other a posteriori avenues for concept acquisition.
- e-pure science – knowledge confirmed by non-empirical methods or a priori sources of evidence.

It is uncertain whether pure natural science is expounded in *Foundations* or lies outside of Kant's book, downstream from it. Suppose that he did expound it there. What kind of pure science is it, then?

Older exegetes sought to argue that it is s-pure knowledge.[76] Specifically, that it is knowledge inferred from ‹matter›, a concept whose *content* is a priori, allegedly, because it is given by explicit definition from space and time, and *they* are a priori representations. These scholars think that perception contributes to pure science just trivially, by securing that ‹matter› refers. Still, that contribution leaves the concept s-pure in the sense above; hence so must be the science that follows from it.

This reading cannot be true. Strong evidence, available early in *Foundations*, speaks against it. Kant, in *Phoronomy*, explains that he means ‹motion› in the sense of temporal change in kinematic relations with respect to some *relative* space. But the latter notion is a posteriori:

> In any experience, something must be sensed – that is the real of the sensible intuition. Hence, the space too (in which we set up our experience of motion) must be *perceptible*. Namely, we must designate it through what can be *sensed*. Now this space, qua container of all objects of experience (and such an object itself) is named the *empirical space*. But this space, being *material*, is itself movable. (481; my emphasis)

In effect, 'relative space' is a concept obtained from sensibility, that is, from perceived volumes of matter in fairly stable configurations. Then it counts as

---

[76] This notion seems to be the key assumption behind Cramer 1985 and Plaass 1994.

s-*impure*; and so do 'force,' 'mass,' and 'action,' the other basic concepts in *Foundations*. Then a theory built on them cannot be s-pure.

Knowledge of Natures

Descartes had reset the terms of natural philosophy by claiming, against the Scholastics, that the nature of body is just extension (with its modes), and nothing else. Newton, Leibniz, Locke and others then demurred that extension is not sufficient to ground a sound physics of body. That Cartesian failure afflicted his posterity with a new and important problem: What is the *nature* of body? And, how might we know it?

Kant in *Foundations* answers it three times over, from distinct vantage points. One is transcendental: A body is an object of outer sense, so it has the properties entailed by that status. Another is metaphysical: A body is a composite material substance; that status yields another set of essential traits. Lastly, from the vantage point of natural philosophy: A body is a proper part of the world, *Weltganz*, qua global system of matter governed by nomic interactions; that too bestows essential properties on body.

In consequence, there are three lists of properties that we may call Kantian accounts of the nature of body. The *t-list*: A body is any object (of outer sense) with numeric attributes, qualitative features that come in degrees, relational properties with causal import, and modally qualifiable states. The *m-list*: A body is anything that is mobile, impenetrable, and movent. The *k-list*: A body is finite extension endowed with velocity of translation, repulsive and attractive forces, linear inertia and momentum, and privileged motion-states. For the remainder of this part, my framing question will be: How does Kant connect his three lists inferentially?

Patterns of Evidential Reasoning

If *Foundations* does not deal in s-pure science, a more promising route opens if we consider the other option: Some natural science might count as epistemologically pure. I go down this path next, to see how far it goes. That is, I present here the patterns of a priori inference available in his doctrine, so as to decide how much of his reasoning they can account for.

Progressive Argument

In deriving some key substantive claims in the book, Kant uses 'proof,' *Beweis*. A strong term, to be sure, but he means it. Some of his proofs really are deductive arguments that progress from secure premises to a desired conclusion. His proof of the Law of Inertia epitomizes this direct-inference approach to evidence. Kant infers the law in *Mechanics*, from premises established upstream from that chapter. The argument structure of his proof is easy to reconstruct:

i. Any change in a matter's state of motion must have a cause.
ii. That cause is either internal or external.
iii. But, it is not internal.
iv. Ergo, causes of motion-change are always external (to the body).

For premise (i), Kant's warrant is dual: He infers it from the Second Analogy and the thesis that matter undergoes change "only through motion." For his proof, however, the crucial step is premise (iii). What makes it true? Kant responds, "matter has no purely internal determinations, nor grounds thereof." He elaborates: The only "inner principles" we are acquainted with whereby a substance changes its *own* state are mentalistic: desire, thought, feeling, and will (544). None are efficient causes of kinematic change. So, there are no internal causes of self-acceleration.

Unfortunately, his premise is false. There *are* inner principles of change in *material* substances, namely, internal forces. Bodies are extended and they have parts that exert forces on each other, *within* the body.[77] So, they count as internal causes – and thus may change the body's motion-state from within. To guarantee that internal forces do not change it, Kant ought to have in place a version of his law of action and reaction. Specifically, he must prove this: In an extended body, all internal forces are pairwise balanced (the action of one is equal and opposite to the action of the other). If he can do so, that fact entails that internal forces induce no net self-acceleration. The latter, in turn, can save his proof of the law above (that all changes of motion-state in a body come from external causes) by giving him a true premise to supplant (iii). Thereby it would keep his argument valid while also making it sound. In any case, extended bodies have two kinds of purely internal grounds of determination. Then he ought to revise his thesis (iii).

Conceptual Analysis

One source of a priori evidence for him appears to be the analysis of privileged concepts in his special metaphysics – for instance, the concept of matter. Analyzing that notion would break it into *Teilbegriffe*, the concepts that make up ‹matter› as its parts, so to say. Then grasping these concept-parts jointly

---

[77] These forces are of two kinds. Some are actions at a distance (e.g., gravity, magnetism) that even spatially separated parts exert on one another. Others are contact forces that any two adjoining body parts mutually exert across their common surface of contact. The modern terms for them are 'body forces' and 'stresses,' respectively.

would amount to knowing the nature of matter. Indeed, Kant at times speaks as if he will analyze that concept: "the understanding reduces [to motion] all the other predicates that *belong to the nature of matter*, and so the science of nature is a doctrine of motion," pure or applied (477, my emphasis).

In *Foundations*, four otherwise mysterious concepts seem particularly amenable to this exegesis. Kant begins his chapters with single 'explications.' Each one bluntly posits a property of matter: mobility, impenetrability, being movent, and having objective motion-states. We may ask Kant why these concepts rather than some others.[78] And, we may ask how he *knows* matter to have these properties universally. To the latter question, I think, he would plausibly answer that he knows it by conceptual analysis. For one, his words elsewhere give more credence to this proposal. Generally, he thinks that metaphysics relies inter alia on a procedure (*Zergliederung*, literally a dis-membering) that takes a concept and breaks it down into components, *Teilbegriffe*; the outcomes of that is analytic judgments. Now as he begins *Foundations*, he announces he will subject the concept ‹matter› to *Zergliederung*. So, it seems reasonable to suppose that 'matter is mobile,' and so on, is inferred by conceptual analysis. For another, even in the Critique he sometimes relied on conceptual analysis to disclose the essence of fundamental entities for him.[79]

At the same time, there is an alternative exegesis; Eric Watkins thinks that knowledge of the four properties above comes not from concept analysis but from transcendental argument. I address his case below.

Analysis-Plus

There is a pattern of inference in *Foundations* that counts as a stronger version of analytic reasoning. It is a stepwise procedure that, at critical junctures, relies on the Principle of Sufficient Reason (PSR) to keep the inference from stalling, and to propel it forward. In essence, those steps are: partial analysis; deduction to a partition class of possible outcomes; appeal to PSR so as to rule out all outcomes but one; then completion of the analysis.

This analytic-plus pattern is the argument structure of Kant's justification for his third law of mechanics. He starts with a *concept*, namely, ‹relative motion›, and I reconstruct his proof as follows.

---

[78] A conjecture: Perhaps he thinks each property is explanatorily basic to the sub-discipline treated in that particular chapter. For example, mobility is key to building a phoronomy; impenetrability to 'dynamics'; exerting momentum to mechanics, and so on. In any case, the interpretive question of why Kant asserted these four properties in particular remains open and in need of further study.

[79] James Messina has shown this to be the case with space, in the Metaphysical Exposition of the First Critique (Messina 2015).

1. Relative motion is a mutual relation between any two interacting bodies.
2. Each body has a respective share [*relativer Anteil*] in that relation.
3. Their individual shares can stand in any proportion to each other.
4. There is no *sufficient reason* [*Grund*] why a body should have a greater respective share than the other.
5. Hence, they interact with *equal* relative motions.
6. Because their motions are equal and opposite, they are endowed with equal and opposite 'movent forces.'
7. Equal forces cause equal actions.
8. Ergo, any two colliding bodies exert equal and opposite actions on each other.

In his inference, steps 2 and 6 count as results of concept analysis.[80] Step 3 is the inference to a partition class of possible outcomes. At that juncture, the train of reasoning would stall – it points to no conclusion univocally – thus Kant restarts the process by invoking the PSR at step 4, so as to conclude to a determinate outcome:

> we are considering the two bodies' motion as determinable merely in absolute space. Now in that space, each body must have an equal share in the motion that one of them had in the relative space [to which we had referred their *apparent* motions]. Their shares must be equal, because *there is no reason* to ascribe to one body a greater share than to the other. (545, my emphasis)

In support of my view about his argument being conceptual-analytic, I point to his words in *Phenomenology*:

> As to Theorem III, to *show the truth* of the equal and mutually-opposed motions [of interacting bodies] ... the mere possibility of dynamical influence (qua property of matter) ... entails that, for any motion of a matter, there always is an equal and opposite motion of the other matter. This follows from the mere *concept of a relative motion*. ... Hence, like anything adequately *provable from mere concepts*, Theorem III is a law of an absolutely necessary counter-motion. (562, my emphasis)

These words strongly suggest that evidence for his Third Law comes from a species of concept analysis. However, he would regard the law as a *synthetic* truth, not analytic – for, in relying on the PSR indispensably, his proof goes beyond mere analysis. Put somewhat differently, it is synthetic because analytic reasoning alone cannot secure his conclusion.

---

[80] Specifically, steps 1 and 2 are a partial analysis of the concept ‹relative motion›, whereas 6 comes from analyzing ‹matter›, being the Explication at the head of chapter III: "Matter is the movable insofar as, qua movable, it has *movent force*" (536).

Analysis-plus was a not uncommon pattern of inference in eighteenth-century foundations of science. Jakob Hermann had first applied it; interestingly, he too used it to infer to the equality of action and reaction, but from a starting point somewhat different from Kant's. Hermann began with the concept of corporeal action (by contact). He *analyzed* it as a struggle between an 'agent' body endowed with 'active force,' and a 'patient' body that puts up a passive force of resistance. To overcome it, the agent could apply more force, less force, or just as much as the patient has force to resist. But, Hermann adds, there is no sufficient reason why the agent should act more than it needs to defeat the patient. Wolff then made the appeal to the PSR explicit. Ergo, action equals reaction:

> In this force of inertia of matter is grounded the law of Nature that *to every action there is an equal and opposite reaction*. For in every action there is a struggle [*luctatio*] between an agent body and a patient one, and without such struggle no action, properly so called, *can be conceived* ... Hence all corporeal action *is* a clash between an agent force and the resistance of the patient.
>
> Action is just the application of some force onto a subject capable of receiving it. The force is applied to that body which resists, withstands, reacts. ... So, in saying that action is equal and contrary to the reaction of the patient, all we mean is: in all corporeal action, *as much of the agent's force is lost as it is gained by the body receiving* the action. (Hermann 1716: 3, 378 f, my emphasis)

> We must *not* take the force of a body to be the same as its action. A body does not act on another with all the force that it has, rather *only to the extent that the other body resists* it. Body A's action on B *consists in* A breaking the resistance of B. Then, when B resists no longer, A will push it along without any effort. (Wolff 1720: §§ 669–71, my emphasis)

This justification then became influential. Leibniz praised it, Wolff took it up and made it his own, Du Châtelet did too, and LeSeur and Jacquier even appended it as a gloss to Newton's law of action and reaction.[81] And, Hermann's analytic-plus approach to evidence for basic laws (with the PSR embedded in it) even inspired Euler and d'Alembert in their respective quests to justify the law of inertia and of action and reaction.

In sum, by resorting to analysis-plus Kant was a man of his rationalist times. The question for interpreters is whether in *Foundations* conceptual analysis is his dominant pattern of inference or just one among many.

---

[81] See the discussion and references in Stan 2013. Thomas LeSeur and François Jacquier were two Minim friars who (assisted by J. L. Calandrini, a Swiss mathematician) reissued the *Principia* with extensive commentaries (1739–42, Geneva, 4 vols.).

Indirect Proofs

Another Kantian source of evidence comes from alternatives to direct argument. *Foundations* relies on two species of indirect reasoning: a proof by *reductio* and an apagogic inference. I reconstruct them below.

To understand the first, it helps to start with an explanation and a reminder. Kant in *Phenomenology* has an idiosyncratic concept, namely, ‹absolute motion›. A piece of matter counts as being in absolute motion if it moves *truly*, its motion is an *actual* kinematic change, and yet the motion does *not* consist in a relation to a material space external to the matter so moving. More plainly put, absolute motion is not a relation between two material relata. "Absolute motion would be that which a body would have without any relation to some other matter. The only motion of this kind would be the rectilinear motion of the *Weltganz*, that is, the system of all matter" (562). The reminder is that he thinks the physical universe, or world-system, has a point W that counts as its center of gravity.[82]

Kant is emphatic that absolute motion is not an object of possible experience; conversely stated, it is an impossible object. This adamant claim is a key premise in his proof by *reductio*.

The proof aims to establish the equality of action and reaction, which he sometimes calls the 'Law of Antagonism,' for it is about two movent forces opposing each other head-on.[83] In a nutshell, his proof says: Any *unequal* action-reaction pair would cause an absolute motion; but the latter is impossible; ergo, action always *equals* reaction. Reconstructed to account for its richness, his indirect proof would go as follows.

1. Suppose that, in a system S of bodies, their mechanical actions on each other are unequal.
2. That would cause S to undergo a net acceleration from within.[84]
3. In turn, that self-acceleration entails a change of state in W.
4. Which change would amount to the *Weltganz* being set in motion.
5. But that change counts as an absolute motion.[85]
6. Absolute motion is impossible.

Ergo, action must equal reaction.

---

[82] I discussed the point W in Section I. Recall, Kant regards it as the origin of the privileged frame of reference that he calls 'absolute space.' However, Kantian absolute motion is *not* motion in regard to absolute space.

[83] Nota bene: Kant has two arguments for this principle. One is in *Mechanics*, just under his Third Law, and is a progressive argument whose structure is analysis-plus as I discussed it. The other occurs late in *Phenomenology*.

[84] That is, due to forces exerted by its parts, not to an outside force external to S.

[85] Because there is no matter-frame external to the universe such that the *Weltganz* could count as having been set in motion relative to *it*. Thus *ex suppositione* all the matter we ever experience counts as being 'inside' the universe (is part of it), not external to it.

That makes it a proof by *reductio*: It shows that negating the desired conclusion entails a result known a priori to be false, namely, that absolute motion is a possible object of experience. The reasoning above is my construal of the thought behind his words that

> Any proof of a law of motion is apodictic if it shows that denying the law entails a rectilinear motion of the world-system. It is apodictic just because negating the law would result in absolute motion, which is simply impossible. Such is the Law of Antagonism in any community of matter through motion. For, any deviation (from the equality of action and reaction) would dislodge from its place the common center of gravity of all matter. Thereby, it would displace the world-system. (562 f)

Finally, to see how cogent his line of argument is, I include a diagram that makes his reasoning intuitive (Figure 5). In particular, my diagram serves to clarify his premise (3), which otherwise may seem mysterious.

The second indirect argument stretches over much of *Foundations*. To grasp it, here too we need some preliminaries. By the late 1780s, there were three ontologies for mechanics – three conceptually distinct pictures of the unit body. By that I mean the sub-perceptual ingredient (often called a particle) out of which sensible bodies might be obtained by physical aggregation. Put modernly, these unit ingredients were the mass point, the rigid body, and the deformable continuum.[86] Kant designates their corresponding ontologies by the terms 'physical monadology,' the 'system of absolute impenetrability,' and 'infinitely divisible matter,' respectively. In Appendix B, I explain these objects in detail. Here, to keep my account synoptic, I abbreviate them as follows: P denotes the mass point, R the rigid body, and C the deformable continuum. Against this backdrop, Kant wishes to argue that C is the correct ontology for mechanics. In his words, "matter is divisible to infinity, namely, in parts that are themselves matter."[87] I reconstruct his indirect proof for C as follows.

i. At basic levels, matter is either P or R or C. *Quartum non datur.*
ii. But, not R.
iii. Not P either.
iv. Ergo, C: Matter is infinitely divisible.

---

[86] The term 'particle' is fundamentally equivocal. It can denote any of the three unit ingredients above, but each is conceptually *irreducible* to the others. See Appendix B.

[87] That is Proposition 4 of *Dynamics* (503). Recall, by 'dynamics' he means a theory of matter, just as Leibniz and Wolff did – in particular, the general program that 'force' is constitutive to matter, and so (contra Descartes, d'Alembert, Euler, and their ilk) that the essence of body cannot be just impenetrable extension; force is co-essential with it.

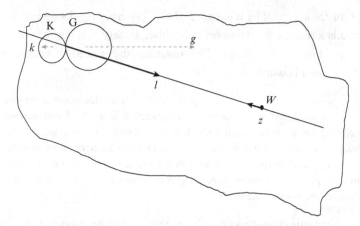

Figure 5 Why unequal action-reaction pairs would cause the mass-center of the physical universe to accelerate. Let K and G be two 'matters.' Let k and g be their mutual but unequal actions, with g greater than k. Let l denote the excess action (of G over K) that results from their interacting causally. And, let W be the mass-center of the 'system of all matter.' If the actions k and g are not equal, l is positive, and then the net linear momentum of the world-whole *increases*. That will cause the center W to accelerate, namely, gain a velocity increment z. (In fact, z equals p/l, where p is the mass of all matter external to the system K-G.) Kant's point is: A velocity like z is not a possible object of experience because it does not consist in a material relation (of W to anything outside the physical universe).

The proof is valid, so I will just survey his warrant for its premises.

In support of premise (ii), Kant accuses that R is explanatorily vacuous: It gives no insight into impenetrability. For such explanatory failures he uses 'occult quality,' a derogatory phrase common among the post-Scholastics. Rigidity is one such quality, he contends: "In fact, absolute impenetrability is no more (and no less) than an occult quality. Ask: What is the cause of matters not being able to penetrate each other in their motion [as they run into one another]? They will answer: Because matters are impenetrable" (502). That may be so. Still, his point is at best a reason to think that premise (ii) above is *illicit* in natural philosophy as he thinks it should be built. But we need to see evidence that (ii) is *false*; that is the real point of contention here, not architectonic legitimacy.

He does give two arguments against R, in a General Remark to Dynamics. They assert that an 'absolutely hard' body cannot exist because it would require two kinds of infinite force – and *those* do not exist. Specifically, he claims that in a true rigid its parts would exert infinite attractive force on one another, and the body would absorb an infinite impulse in any collision.[88]

As to premise (iii), he aims to establish it by showing that P is incoherent; to defenders of P, he refers as 'monadists.'[89] Kant starts from a crucial thesis that he and the monadists share, namely, that "matter fills space by means of repulsive force." He *thinks* the thesis entails a key corollary. Namely, that in a filled volume every part of it contains force that repels every other part around it in *every* direction, away from itself. Ergo, that every part in that volume is movable independently (of these other parts), and so is *every point* within these parts: "In a filled space, there can be *no* point that does not *itself* exert repulsion in *every* direction, ... hence it is movable *on its own*" (504, my emphasis).

However, this alleged entailment (the independent mobility of every point in a filled space) contradicts P, for in a volume made up of physical monads, *not* every point in it can move independently of any other. Only some points can, namely, the discrete points where a particular monad's mass and source of forces (of attraction and repulsion) are located. The corollary thus "leaves the monadist with no way out" (504). Ergo, C alone is left standing: Matter is a physical continuum.[90]

The few exegetes who have studied this aspect of Kant's theory of matter agree about the overall shape of his above inference against physical monads, but they are not hopeful about its validity.[91] His argument for the physical continuum thus appears less than conclusive. Ultimately, then, Kant put indirect proof to divergent ends, sometimes to overdetermine a case (for Law III) and sometimes to leave it underdetermined (e.g., his picture of matter).

---

[88] *Foundations*, 549. These arguments are hard to assess. They are lapidary and couched in obsolete Leibnizian terms from the 1690s (e.g., 'moment' and 'solicitation') that were always fuzzy and equivocal. In particular, Kant does not signal if his terms denote infinitesimal or integral quantities, instantaneous or temporally extended. That frustrates the attempt to evaluate the first. Moreover, the argument risks begging the question: It assumes that rigid bodies have internal forces, but the supporters of that ontology denied it (in a rigid body, internal stresses are not a well-defined notion; see Appendix B). The second argument is not new with him.

[89] That is because 'physical monads' are a species of mass-points, the ontology that I abbreviated above as P. Thus, Kant in *Foundations* argues against the very picture of matter he used to hold in the 1750s.

[90] This train of reasoning occurs in his proof of Proposition 4 of *Dynamics* (the thesis of infinite divisibility) and in the subsequent Remark 1.

[91] The culprit is a non sequitur: From 'a volume is filled by repulsive force' it does not follow – as Kant thinks – that every point there is movable independently (of *every other point* in it). Only *some* points in that volume must be so movable (for it to be impenetrable). But a physical monadist can accept the latter implication. Physical monads are independently movable points causing repulsive force around them, and so they can satisfy Kant's starting premise. For critical discussion, see Friedman (2013: 149ff).

Transcendental Argument

Dissatisfaction with 'substitutionist' readings of *Foundations* led Eric Watkins to claim that Kant's master argument there is transcendental.[92]

Specifically, it has two stages. The first "establishes the most basic feature of matter." That is, it infers that mobility (qua universal property of matter) is the most basic condition of possibility for experience of objects in outer sense. At the second stage, new transcendental arguments infer to the *properties* of space-filling, movent force, and true state (of motion) as further conditions for that experience. Finally, a last round of transcendental argument aims to establish *principles*: the various propositions that he calls theorems and laws. Kant derives each principle from one of the four properties of matter (Watkins 2019: 78–80).

This reading is quite recent, and scholars no doubt will take it up to engage with it soon. In anticipation of that stage, I offer three general remarks meant to suggest further lines of discussion.

First remark: If indeed *Foundations* establishes conditions of possible experience, we may wonder about the exact meaning of that term. There are two senses to it, and they pull the account in different directions. (1) It could denote our experience of the *manifest* image of the world: be it as episodic cognitions, namely, casual, pre-theoretical acquaintance with everyday objects; or as loosely connected propositions inferred by induction from the patterns and regularities given at mesoscales, in perception. (2) Or it could refer to experience of the world as given in the *scientific* image. We may call it 'exact,' and with good reason: Exact experience has key traits that experience in the manifest image lacks.[93]

Briefly put, exact experience is *precise:* It forms an ensemble of quantitative statements, devised to let us infer from data to predictions; or to explananda stated in terms of mathematized properties. And it is *strongly connected*: A set of propositional items linked to one another, directly or indirectly, by inferential and explanatory connections. Finally, it is *theoretical*: Its fundamental vocabulary is non-perceptual concepts, related to perceptibles via lawlike principles.[94]

---

[92] 'Substitutionist' readings took Kant's main concepts there to result from instantiating categories (by applying them to matter) and inserting the resulting output into the statements of Kant's Analogies of Experience, so as to obtain his three Laws of Mechanics. For a statement and refutation, see Watkins (2019: 72–7), which goes back to 1998.

[93] The duality between the manifest and the scientific image of the world is a theme from Wilfrid Sellars; cf. his "Philosophy and the Scientific Image of Man." The main difference between these images is in their sources of evidence, rigor of assemblage, and reliance on theoretical terms and entities: Only the scientific image deals in them.

[94] Here is an illustration. Newton's *Principia* is a quantitative theory of four theoretical terms: 'force,' 'mass,' 'space distance,' and 'time length.' To each corresponds a parameter (f, m, s, and t) that we can access empirically *only* via theory-mediated measurements – not directly, by

Returning to Watkins' thesis (that the book is a transcendental argument), I suggest that his case enjoys different degrees of plausibility, depending on how we construe 'experience.' Suppose he means it in sense (1). That reading has two consequences worth addressing. It seems to imply that the First Critique is incomplete: The concepts and principles of the Transcendental Analytic are *not* sufficient to account for the possibility of experience. Rather, they need supplementing with the *Foundations'* concepts and principles – and only then does Kant have a complete explanation of possible experience. And it appears to imply that, before Newton, no one had genuine experience because they lacked knowledge of the kinematic structures and mechanical laws that Kant (following Newton's results) vindicated in his book. That may be too strong a consequence. Suppose that matter really has the essence and causal dispositions that Aristotelian-Scholastic physics ascribed to it.[95] Then the principles of that physics would be enough to explain experience of the world as given in the manifest image. After all, Aristotelian physics was *the* science of the world as given to common sense. So, the inventory of concepts and laws in *Foundations* appears needlessly strong.

Second remark: Suppose now that Watkins means his exegesis to be about determinate experience in sense of (2). Before we assess this particular interpretation, we must ask if Kant thinks that conditions of possibility must be necessary, sufficient, or both. The point matters, because his listed conditions (for determinate experience of material nature) are just nearly sufficient; they are not entirely sufficient for the task.[96] And, they are *not* necessary. That is because there is another list of conditions, which differs in makeup from his list, and yet it entails just as much empirical content as his. Consider this alternative list of conditions for determinate experience:

- concepts – motion qua change of generalized coordinate; virtual work; kinetic energy; conservative potential.
- laws – the Principle of Virtual Work; d'Alembert's Principle.
- phenomenology – a motion is actual if any two Euclidean observers see it as having the same relevant quantity.

---

unaided pre-theoretical perception (as we access objects and events in the manifest image). The theory-mediated part is crucial and does serious explanatory work; for a detailed account of that work in Newtonian dynamics, cf. Smith 2014. I am indebted to the late George E. Smith for deeply illuminating discussions on this topic.

[95] Bear in mind that pre-modern physics is radically at odds with Kant's foundation. For instance, that physics lacked the law of inertia, the Newtonian notion of force, any concept of interaction, and the Galilean kinematics of *Phoronomy*. Aristotelian premodern physics was internally coherent, weakly quantitative, and empirically adequate, just not to the extent of Galileo-Newton dynamics. But the issue here is whether *ordinary* experience needs the latter dynamics in some indispensable respect.

[96] I explain why in Stan 2023.

This list is the conceptual basis of analytic mechanics, a stronger alternative to Newton that Lagrange began to develop in the 1770s at the Berlin Academy. The Lagrangian basis accounts for at least as much experience as *Foundations* can. To sum up the problem: Kant's inventory of conditions for determinate experience is optional, and so it cannot be necessary, because we can do without them. Now proponents of the transcendental-argument construal assert that it "reveals the necessary conditions" for experience of matter in space (Watkins 2019: 78). This delicate aspect deserves further discussion, then.

Third remark: It would be good to try and clarify the structure of transcendental arguments in *Foundations*. Notoriously, when they occur in the Critique, such arguments have proven quite recalcitrant to logical elucidation.[97] Until then, we are not in a position to know just how good Kant's inferences in natural philosophy are. In addition, another aspect (beyond logical structure) needs clarification as well, namely, whether the concepts established by transcendental arguments *must* be a priori, or semantically pure. In the Critique, they are: space, time, and the categories. However, in *Foundations*, concepts secured by such inferences – for example, the attributes making up the essence of matter – are empirical, not a priori; and Kant is candid about that status.[98]

To conclude, the exegesis of *Foundations* as a transcendental argument deserves serious attention; I have tried above to suggest lines of inquiry as we engage further with Watkins' hermeneutic proposal.

Constructions

Another source of evidence for him is construction. We may expect *ab initio* that construction does work in *Foundations*; after all, the book is about mathematizing nature, and Kant famously thought that construction was the paradigm of knowledge acquisition in mathematics. And, to be sure, a number of scholars have used constructivist language to clarify his arguments there – a move he seemed to encourage himself:

---

[97] There are three broad views on their structure, as follows. Let P be a claim to be established. On the progressive view, a transcendental argument is a deductive inference that concludes to P (Bennett 1966; Strawson 1966). On the regressive view, P explains some accepted fact, e.g., our having empirical knowledge. Presumably, then, a regressive transcendental argument is an abductive inference to P as the best explanation of that fact. That seems to be the view behind Ameriks 1978. Lastly, the third view implies transcendental arguments are in fact *descriptions* of a chain of transmission that begins with an acquired right (as the first link in the chain) and ends with the right to assert P. I take that to be the implicit, unstated view behind the interpretation in Henrich 1989.

[98] To be sure, the knowledge claims corresponding to these concepts (viz. 'matter is mobile,' 'is impenetrable,' etc.) *are* a priori. However, by Kant's own admission, the concepts themselves – mobility, impenetrability, inertia, movent force – are empirical.

Kant's Natural Philosophy 55

> In regard to *physica generalis* – the pure part of natural science, where they commonly mix metaphysical and mathematical constructions – I thought it necessary to present the former in a system, together with the principles for the construction of these concepts – thereby presenting the very possibility of a mathematical science of nature. (4: xiv)

However, constructivist exegeses (aided by Kant's occasional non-standard use of the term) have led to semantic proliferation: 'Construction' has come to denote several procedures. Hence, first I must disambiguate the term before I examine its role in *Foundations*.[99] Accordingly, we may distinguish these senses. *K-construction*: to instantiate some non-empirical concept by ostension in pure intuition. Characteristic output: a singular representation that refers directly. *E-construction*: to bring about a figure or diagram by compass and straightedge. Output: a regular figure as in Euclid's *Elements*; or a combination of them. *S-construction*: to replace intermediate steps (in a proof by diagrammatic reasoning) with discursive-algebraic inference. Output: a shorter proof. *F-construction*: to locate a privileged 'relative space' by iterative application of Kant's three laws of mechanics, plus universal gravity. Output: a frame of reference with the origin at the mass-center of some system of bodies. *M-construction*: to construct metaphysically. An obscure procedure whose exact mechanism no one has explained clearly, let alone defended. I discuss it below, but first, a clarification.

I defined k-construction from the standpoint of Kant's cognitive semantics. To supplement his insight, we can also define it by listing the operations on which it must rely. A k-construction always iterates one or more of these procedures: building a diagram by compass and straightedge; generating a figure by the motion of mathematical points, lines or surfaces; diagrammatic reasoning; and the rule-governed manipulation of algebraic symbols. This makes it clear that e-constructing and s-constructing are just species of k-construction. Euclidean constructing allowed *nothing but* compass and straightedge.[100] Symbolic construction was just an intermediate step in an inferential chain that *always* ended in a diagram: Once found, the solutions

---

[99] I use prefixes for easier tracking of these senses. 'K' denotes Kant's official sense of construction; 'S' is symbolic, 'E' is Euclidean, 'M' is metaphysical, and 'F' is for the construction-type that Friedman has attributed to Kant.

[100] Euclid's Postulates I–III licensed two elementary constructions: to draw a line between any two points (by straightedge) and a circle around any point (by compass). These acts could then be reiterated at will, to generate non-elementary objects, e.g., a triangle. Subsequently, Proclus allowed that any figure may be drawn by motion, viz., may be regarded as the orbit of a moving point, line or plane surface. Hobbes and Kant followed Proclus in this 'kinematic' account of geometric concept-instantiation. For Kant's views of motion as generating act for geometric objects, see Pollok 2006.

(constructed symbolically) had to be presented geometrically, by compass and straightedge in pure intuition.[101]

In contrast, 'metaphysical construction' is not part of Kant's official inventory of concepts and methods, so an exegesis that saddles him with it must earn its right to do so. I believe that, in attributing it to him, Plaass and others misread his words – in particular, the passage (at 4: xiv) I cited above.[102] The passage *seems* to commit Kant to metaphysical constructions having a place in mathematical physics. But it is just a slip of syntax in his phrasing. A more reasonable version of it is: "In regard to *physica generalis* – where they mix metaphysical *concepts* and mathematical constructions – I thought it necessary to present the former (the metaphysical) *concepts* in a system, together with the principles for the construction of *these* concepts" (4: xiv; my emphasis). Correctly read, then, Kant is committed to there being *mathematical* constructions for metaphysical *concepts*. Namely, he thinks that a procedure of mathematics (constructing) can take as inputs *non*mathematical representations, supplied by metaphysics. I have not seen any evidence that he thinks there is a procedure that counts as a proper species of constructing – namely, as instantiating a concept a priori in pure intuition – and yet it is nonmathematical, purely metaphysical.

If I am right, then mathematical constructions of distinctly metaphysical concepts are easy to detect, because they must contain diagrammatic reasoning, which is the mark of constructions as he means it. In *Foundations*, there are two instances of that: composition of motions in Phoronomy, and the 'communication of motion' in Mechanics. I take this chance to examine the latter, so as to answer three questions. How does the constructing work, precisely? Does it yield synthetic a priori knowledge? And how much can it explain?

'Communication of motion' is his phrase for momentum exchanges in an interaction. It is a causal process that is symmetric, temporally extended though brief, and results in changes to the velocities of any two corporeal substances involved in communication of motion. By constructing that process, Kant means to give a mathematical procedure that enables us to predict

---

[101] Symbolic construction replaced known quantities (a given length, area, volume, or angle size) by a letter, or 'symbol.' Given relations between these 'symbolic' quantities were then expressed via the common algebraic symbols '+,' '−,' '÷,' '×,' etc. The generic task was to infer to an unknown quantity (say, x) by rearranging the symbolic terms in these expressions, as licensed by the operator rules of elementary algebra. Symbolic constructions, in the sense that Kant had in mind, were intermediary steps in a process of deriving the solution to a polynomial equation. For explanations, see Shabel 1998.

[102] Miller & Miller claim that metaphysical construction is "akin to, but distinct from" mathematical construction, and uses "mathematics-like" outputs (1994: 64, 127). Plaass thought metaphysical construction was nonmathematical, but he never explained what it consists in – what structure it had, allegedly.

the exit velocities of two colliding bodies, if we know their masses and relative speed: "in the community of the two bodies, the effect is constructed as follows."[103]

There follows a diagram and some reasoning on it (546). His drawing is a palimpsest – it flattens into one figure three distinct, consecutive stages of momentum transfer. So, I must disentangle his reasoning (and tacit premises) by presenting it as the three separate diagrams that he had in mind and should have drawn separately. I do that next; recall, his construction is of a very specific process, namely, the direct inelastic impact of two solids.[104]

First, he uses geometry to construct the initial conditions, that is, the masses and relative speeds of the colliding bodies. Instead of constructing mass, however, he constructs a mass *ratio* of the two bodies about to collide. To that representational end, he uses area: For the two disks in Figures 6 and 7, their areas have the same ratio as the masses of the bodies they stand for. And, relative speed is constructed as the distance *ab* between the disks' geometric centers (Figure 6).

The next stage constructs the bodies' true speeds. For that, Kant divides the relative-speed segment *ab* in two parts, whose lengths are *inversely* proportional to the disk areas. Hence, by implication, to the masses of the colliding bodies.

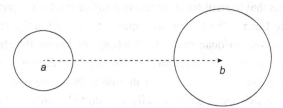

Figure 6 Kant's representation (by geometric construction) of mass ratio and relative speed in the direct collision of two bodies.

---

[103] This remark signals the beginning of his construction, but its surrounding envelope may confuse the reader. The context is his account of the Third Law of Mechanics (546). Now that account is in two parts. One is a proof that, in collision, action equals reaction. The proof is purely *discursive* and relies on no construction at all – I explained it above, under 'Analysis-Plus.' The other part *is* a geometric constructive procedure: He derives exit velocities (in soft-body impact) by diagrammatic reasoning. But, to carry it out, Kant needs his Third Law – it is a crucial premise for it – and so he had to secure it in advance.

[104] A collision is direct (or head-on) if the bodies' velocities are on the line between their mass centers; otherwise, it is oblique. It is inelastic if the two bodies move together (at the same speed) post impact; if they rebound, it is elastic. For unknown reasons, Kant just treats solid masses, but fluids (liquids and gases) can collide too. It is far from clear that *Foundations* has the resources to account for *that*. Which again raises the question of just how general his foundation is.

58   *The Philosophy of Immanuel Kant*

Figure 7 Kant's representation (by geometric construction) of his idea that bodies have true speeds in collision.

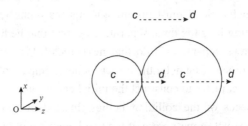

Figure 8 Kant's representation (by geometric construction) of the exit speeds of two bodies post impact – the outcome of their frontal collision.

That is, $ac/bc = m_B/m_A$. The constructed output of this stage is two collinear segments (Figure 7):[105]

The last step constructs the *Wirkung* of the communicated motion. Kant claims that, when the collision is over, the bodies remain at rest. But that outcome is visible just in the mass-center frame, relative to which they have the true speeds ac and bc in Figure 6 (that is, the frame with the origin at c). Thus, he infers that to an observer at rest in a *different* relative space – namely, the lab frame $Oxyz$ – the bodies will appear to move jointly, at a common speed. That unknown quantity is the *Wirkung*, or kinematic effect of their interaction by means of mutual movent forces; determining it was the real point of asking for communication of motion to be constructed. And so, he constructs their exit speed geometrically, as a dotted segment cd equal to the *pre-collision* speed of c, the common mass center of the two bodies as observed in the lab frame $Oxyz$ (Figure 8).[106] Superimpose these three constructions, *mutatis mutandis*, and we obtain his cryptic diagram from *Foundations*.

---

[105] Why collinear? Because of his theory of true motion. It claims that, when two bodies interact, their true motion consists in a relation of *mutual* approach (i.e., of change in relative distance along ab) and that their individual true speeds are 'shares' in this mutual relation, hence they are parts of ab. Cf. Section I again, for a full explanation.

[106] Why does the bodies' *post*-collision speed equal the mass-center's *pre*-collision speed? Because, after impact, they come to rest relative to the mass-center frame; and because the equality of action and reaction – the Third Law that Kant had just proved, before constructing the impact outcome – entails as an easy corollary that the speed of the mass-center itself (the point c, in his diagram) does not change as a result of the two bodies acting on each other. This had been known since Huygens and Newton.

Kant's Natural Philosophy

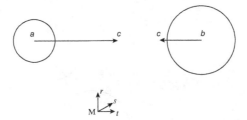

Figure 9 Kant's representation (by geometric construction) of the individual 'movent forces' [*bewegende Kräfte*] of two bodies before impact.

But what *metaphysical* concepts did he just construct geometrically? There are two such notions at issue in his diagram: corporeal action and movent force. The former is part of the matter-concept at the core of his metaphysics, and the latter is a metaphysical determination of matter.[107] Movent force gets constructed as an area and a segment (Figure 9). It is because Kant assumes that the measure of movent force is the product $m\mathbf{v}$, namely, mass times *true* velocity.

However, the former concept (mechanical action) is more elusive. He mentions it briefly – by means of discursive judgments, not an intuitive construction – in his exposition of Law III. In any communication of motion (by impact), two bodies always collide with equal movent forces, and so they cause each other to stop moving and remain at rest. That is the action: "their [true] motions are equal and opposite, so the two bodies bring each other to rest relative to each other," when observed in their mass-center frame (546). Unfortunately, he forgets to construct his verbal reasoning above. He should have done it as follows (Figure 10):

Above, M*rst* is the frame in which the bodies' common center of mass is at rest before their collision; Kant calls it 'absolute space.'[108]

Now we know how constructing mathematically a metaphysical concept works, in his account. Let us check the epistemic credentials of the knowledge

---

[107] We can put things more exactly. The former concept is mechanical action. Kantian matter is causally active by means of mutual powers; mechanics singles out as basic the power to communicate motion, viz. transfer momentum. Any actual exercise of this basic power counts as an action, i.e., a *mechanical action*. The latter concept is the metaphysical property counting as explanatorily basic in mechanics. Recall the Explication at the head of his Metaphysical Foundations of Mechanics: "Matter is the mobile such that, qua mobile, it has *movent force*."

[108] Note that the frame is in relative motion with respect to the frame O*xyz* to which the initial conditions (qua input-data for the constructing procedure) are referred. I.e., the two spaces have a mutual speed, equal to *cd.*, relative to each other. Recall, the initial conditions are the bodies' masses and their *apparent* motions. Relative to O*xyz*, before impact, B appears at rest and A appears to move toward B at a speed *ab*. Quantitatively, these apparent motions are quite different from their *true* motions.

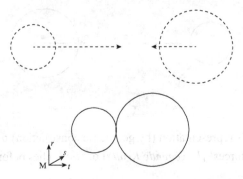

Figure 10 Kant's representation (by geometric construction) of the outcome of two-body collision – namely, mutual rest – as seen by an observer in the mass-center frame.

coming out of it. It is synthetic, to be sure; the indispensable reliance on geometric procedures ensures that its output is ampliative and evidentially dependent on syntheses in intuition. But is it a priori?

I doubt it. To see my point, consider three questions. First, why do his colliding bodies come to mutual rest? Recall his answer: "their motions are equal and opposite, so the bodies bring each other to rest" (546). But that is too brief to be acceptable. In head-on impact, *four* outcomes are possible: mutual rest, elastic rebound, fracture, and plastic flow.[109] There is *no* a priori reason to prefer his official outcome over the others. Not without further premises, anyway – particular ones, of limited range, and given by *experiment*, not by metaphysical reasoning. So, Kant's construction tacitly relies on an empirical premise chosen on mysterious grounds.

Second, why construct the concept of movent force as he did? That is, why let $m\mathbf{v}$ be its measure? In his time, there were two other measures for a body's capacity to effect mechanical changes by moving (which is the property that 'movent force' denotes). Namely, they were *vis viva*, or twice the kinetic energy ($m\mathbf{v}^2$), and also *vis impressa*, or Newtonian force ($md\mathbf{v}/dt$). There is no a priori conclusive reason to prefer $m\mathbf{v}$, the quantity that Kant chose for the notion of 'movent force' in his mechanics.[110] If he had any such reason and it was suitably pure, or non-empirical, Kant kept it well hidden from the reader.

Third, is Kant's construction general? Does it apply to any other case of momentum exchange beyond collisions? He certainly thinks it does: Impact

---

[109] In elastic impact, bodies rebound and regain their shape. Fracture breaks them into pieces – how many, and how they move post collision, was not answerable until the 1920s. Plastic bodies mix into a new shape; or they re-separate with changed shapes and speeds. Finally, inelastic collision (Kant's official case) is when bodies after impact move at the same speed.

[110] As had Wolff in the 1730s, with his notion of *vis motrix*.

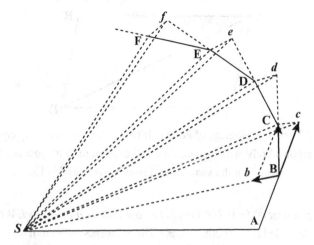

Figure 11 Communicating motion to a body in orbit. At every point, the motion of body A is the effect of two actions: its inertia, which drives it uniformly ahead; and a force of attraction induced by S. These actions compose, and the result is a motion (by the body, from one place to the next, in its orbit). For example, when A arrives at place B, its inertial endeavor Bc compounds with Bb, the action of gravity at that location. Their composite action is BC, which moves the body to place C, over one instant. To construct the composite action, apply the Parallelogram Rule: BC is equal and collinear to the diagonal of the parallelogram formed by the two generating actions Bb, Bc. Over time, this continually reiterated compounding causes the planetary orbit ABCDEF. From Newton 1687: 37.

"differs from communicating motion by attraction just in regard to the direction in which matters resist each other" in their motion (547). Let us consider what it takes to construct their actions in that case. Take two bodies S and B exerting mutual attractive forces as they orbit each other. (The geometric treatment of that process comes from Newton; see Figure 11.)

There is a crucial step in that construction: To infer how either body moves from one instant to the next, we must introduce Composition of Forces as an explicit premise (see Figure 11). Another name for that premise is the Parallelogram of Forces: When two forces act on a body, their joint action is kinematically equivalent – they communicate the same total motion – as a single force given by the diagonal of the parallelogram they form with each other.[111] Constructed geometrically, the rule is as follows (Figure 12).

---

[111] That is, the strength of their resultant, or 'composed force,' equals the diagonal's length, and the force is in the direction of that diagonal.

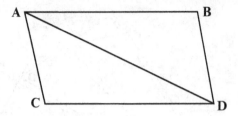

Figure 12 The Parallelogram of Forces. If two forces, respectively equal to AB and AC, act on a body at an instant, they will cause it to move just as a force AD would, in the same time. From Newton 1687: 13.

Now for a crucial fact: *The Parallelogram Rule is a posteriori*. It counts as 'impure' knowledge in both senses: The concepts behind it are acquired notions, not a priori representations; and the warrant for it is empirical, not a priori. In consequence, constructions that rely on the parallelogram rule count as empirical too. Kant had already granted the point, tacitly:

> For the construction of concepts, we require that the condition for presenting them not be borrowed from experience. So, their construction must not presuppose certain *forces*, whose existence can be inferred only from experience. Put more generally: the condition for constructing must not be itself a concept that *cannot at all be given a priori in intuition*. Such are the concepts of cause and *effect*, *action* and resistance, etc. (486 f; my emphasis).

But force, effect [*Wirkung*], and action [*Handlung*] are central concepts in his account of how we construct communication of motion. *Res ipsa loquitur*, then: The generic synthesis that constructs momentum exchanges geometrically must rely indispensably on empirical premises. Which makes his constructed outcome, or result, count as a posteriori knowledge.

The three questions I grappled with above point to a common lesson: m-constructions result in 'impure' knowledge. They require a posteriori concepts (inter alia), and they are not completable without resort to premises made true by empirical evidence.

The same holds of f-constructions, even more so. They too move, by mathematical reasoning, from empirical data (given by observation in astronomy) to claims about locating the reference of an empirical, a posteriori concept, namely, the mass-center qua origin of a theoretically privileged frame of reference.[112] In sum, neither m- nor f-constructions culminate in *pure*

---

[112] In a system of bodies, their mass-center is the point M given by the formula $\sum m_i \mathbf{r}_i = 0$. In words: The point whose distance from each body is inversely proportional to that body's mass.) To locate M for a set of actual bodies, we must infer their masses, from the *empirical* forces on them and the *empirically* given accelerations the forces induce.

intuitions – the indispensable evidence for knowledge that is both ampliative and also apodictic, which he requires of pure natural science. And so, speaking in a normative register, only k-construction (and its species) has the required legitimacy to account for there being any pure natural science as Kant meant it. But there are no k-constructions in *Foundations*.

That is just as well. If metaphysical concepts could be mathematically constructed to yield genuine a priori knowledge, that would be in tension with Kant's tenet in the Critique that mathematics and metaphysics are distinct, for they rely on distinct, non-transferrable methods. My reading of construction in his natural philosophy is compatible with his tenet.

This scrutiny of the evidential work that constructing does in *Foundations* goes beyond Kant's picture of body; it has implications for his philosophy of mathematics too. It shores up the case that he endorsed the Compensation Thesis of the character of mathematics, namely, the view that constructions are indispensable for *inference* in mathematics: Diagrammatic reasoning (on a constructed figure) justifies certain acts of passing from one step to the next in a proof. Thereby construction compensates for the expressive lacunas of eighteenth-century deductive logics. As I showed above, Kant thought inferring to certain quantitative claims (e.g., about exit velocities in two-body collision) cannot be represented by way of discursive reasoning alone. Rather, it needs help from evident features of constructed diagrams.[113]

Conclusions

In natural philosophy, Kant was the last early modern: He grappled with the same foundational problems they had struggled with. The new science created in the seventeenth century required philosophers to decide whether true *motion* is absolute or relative; to know what the nature of *matter* might be; to discover the *laws* that govern all bodies, and explain how a principle might govern inanimate objects; to shed light on how we *quantify* matter and motion, which the new science began to do with increasing success; and to elucidate the *evidential* reasoning that justifies the philosophical basis of that science. Kant took them all up.

In particular, I have argued for the following theses. Kant claimed true motion to be a special relation between interacting bodies; it has causal import (it affects the interaction outcome), so he singled it out. At first he endorsed a picture of matter as discrete, namely, assembled from mass points; then he

---

[113] Two strong defenses of the Compensation Thesis are Friedman (1992: 66–80) and Hogan 2020. The latter uniquely relies on contextual evidence from Kant's time and body of work. I have tried to support the thesis by the same route as Hogan.

switched to the view that matter is continuous, or infinitely divisible. He thought that three laws are privileged – on evidential and explanatory grounds – so he placed them at the foundation of mechanics. He took matter and motion to be quantifiable because we can represent them indirectly by geometric means, which in his broader doctrine underwrite most quantitative inferences. And, he believed mechanics had a basis that counts as a priori, because he aimed to confirm it through non-empirical patterns of argument.

Descartes first struggled with these problems. Then his posterity took them up, in part or as a whole, from Huygens and Newton to Locke and Leibniz, Malebranche and du Châtelet, Wolff and d'Alembert. In the mid 1780s, Kant wrestled with essentially the same questions that had consumed Descartes in his *Principles of Philosophy*.

This fact teaches us late-moderns a few lessons. First, those problems turned out to be unexpectedly hard. In terms of depth and strength of its results, the new science soon exceeded all early expectations for it, and yet making philosophical sense of its basis defied Europe's best minds for two centuries. A sharp disparity in epistemic advances, to be sure. Second, Kant as a natural philosopher grappled with a list of problems that go well beyond the questions raised by Newton's famous book, the *Principia*, and its immediate posterity. Which calls on us historians to expand our perspective on Kant beyond the Marburg-School line of exegesis, while acknowledging its merits and achievements. Third, the science that he had reflected on kept evolving after 1800, in ways that matter to its philosophical foundations. For instance, its mathematical basis changed radically after him, as did its basic dynamical laws. Which means that his official doctrines in *Foundations* cannot be the last word on the Kantian picture of classical physics' impact on philosophy. Rather, the implications of that world-making *Ereignis* remain a live problem for us interpreters.

Appendix A

Measuring Mass and Quantity of Matter

Here I present the results needed to grasp my notion that acceleration is a proxy measure for mass; and also Friedman's exegesis of the idea that, to estimate a body's 'quantity of matter,' we must rely on *its* quantity of *motion*, as Kant has it: "quantity of substance must be estimated only mechanically, or via the quantity of its own motion" (541).

To keep my account easy to follow, I use as examples Jupiter and Europa, its satellite. Let m denote inertial mass, Q quantity of matter, $\mathbf{a}$ acceleration, $\mathbf{p}$ Kant's 'quantity of motion' (i.e., linear momentum), $\mathbf{f}$ impressed force, and $\mathbf{g}$ the force of gravity. Let k, l denote constants, and '≈' indicate proportionality. Here are the relevant facts.

The mass of Jupiter is proportional to the acceleration it induces on Europa by exerting an impressed force on it:

$$m_{\text{Jupiter}} \approx \mathbf{a}_{\text{Europa}} \qquad (1).$$

This is the key result for *my* account of mass having a measure-by-proxy. Further, Jupiter's mass is also proportional to the acceleration of *Jupiter*, caused whenever Europa (or any other body, for that matter) acts on it:

$$m_{\text{Jupiter}} \approx \mathbf{a}_{\text{Jupiter}} \qquad (2).$$

This relation vindicates Kant's claim about estimating the quantity of a substance from its own motion.

In support of Friedman's account, two nomic facts. The *quantity of matter* in Jupiter is proportional to the acceleration it causes in its moon:

$$Q_{\text{Jupiter}} \approx \mathbf{a}_{\text{Europa}} \qquad (3).$$

Finally, that same quantity is proportional to the acceleration that Jupiter suffers under gravity from Europa:[1]

$$Q_{\text{Jupiter}} \approx \mathbf{a}_{\text{Jupiter}} \qquad (4).$$

---

[1] *Nota bene*: In every case above, a different constant of proportionality is at work. Namely, we can transform each expression into an equality, if we multiply the right side by a constant. E.g., (1) becomes $m_{\text{Jupiter}} = k \cdot \mathbf{a}_{\text{Europa}}$, where k equals $(G \cdot \mathbf{g}) / (Q_{\text{Europa}} \cdot r^2)$, whereas (2) needs a different constant, l, to be turned into an equality.

Here is why the relations (1)–(4) are true. They fall out of three laws of nature. The laws are, respectively, $\mathbf{f} = m\mathbf{a}$; $\mathbf{f}_1 = -\mathbf{f}_2$; and $\mathbf{g} \approx Q_1 \cdot Q_2$. Start with his Third Law, namely, that all impressed forces come in pairs, are seated in distinct bodies, and are equal and opposite:

$$\mathbf{f}_{\text{body A on body B}} = -\mathbf{f}_{\text{body B on body A}}.$$

Recall that any impressed force is governed by Newton's second law:

$$\mathbf{f}_{\text{any other body, on A}} = m_{\text{body A}} \cdot \mathbf{a}_{\text{body A}}.$$

Now substitute this equality into the Third Law above, group like terms together, and leave out the signs; they don't matter here. We get:

$$m_A/m_B = \mathbf{a}_B/\mathbf{a}_A.$$

Which entails, as a trivial corollary, the key relations (1) and (2) above.

The Equivalence Principle

Recall how Friedman construes Kant's account of a measuring procedure for mass universally applicable to any object in the world. We start with the availability of weighing, an earthbound procedure that yields a measure for bodies around us. Subsequently, we extend this procedure well beyond its narrow reach (land-based weighing relies on balances or analogous human artifacts). To weigh at cosmic scales, we resort to "projecting the static quantity of terrestrial weight into the heavens by means of the theory of universal gravitation." Thereby, we turn the quantification of matter (by weight) into "a universal measure of quantity of matter for all bodies whatsoever, regardless of their relation to the surface of the earth" (Friedman 2012: 482, 493). In effect, we use gravity – specifically, the motion-changes it produces in all bodies – to infer their masses wherever they are, well beyond the earth. Since weighing (the local variant of this procedure) uses terrestrial gravity to disclose the mass of objects in a balance, measuring mass by means of universal gravity amounts to a *generalized weighing*, as it were: We can weigh stars and galaxies from the motion-effects of universal gravity on them.

A subtlety is weaved into this account. Weighing does *not* measure mass – not directly, anyway. Weighing discloses Q, the quantity of matter as heavy, or responsive to gravitational force acting on it. In weighing an object, we measure its *weight*. Kant has a good grasp of it: The "endeavor to move in the direction of greater gravity is weight" (518). In sum, weight and mass are distinct concepts. Weight is the (invariant) quantity Q of matter qua heavy: the strength of its tending toward any attraction force-center. Mass is the quantity m of its resistance to any impressed force whatsoever. And so, the proper expression for the force of gravity $\mathbf{f_g}$ between any two bodies A and B is in terms of their quantities of heavy matter, Q_A and Q_B, not mass:

$$\mathbf{f_g} \approx (Q_A \cdot Q_B) / r^2.$$

But if weighing measures weight, and weight is not mass, then why is it legitimate to weigh – or infer from gravity effects on – anything as a way to measure *mass*?

There is a universal fact that legitimizes it. Namely, a body's quantity Q of matter happens to be *equal* to its inertial mass m. The claim that this equality holds for all bodies is known as the Weak Equivalence Principle. This principle is a posteriori knowledge: the evidence for it comes from empirical facts. Newton discovered it in 1685 and confirmed it by a double-pendulum experiment; Bessel and Eötvös confirmed it too, the latter from a novel experimental approach.[2]

In sum, Kant's adopting the Newtonian procedure for measuring mass universally relies on three a posteriori premises: the Second Law; the law that gravity is universal, direct at a distance, and proportional to the product of the bodies' respective quantity of matter Q; and the Weak Equivalence Principle.

---

[2] For lucid accounts and analyses of Newton's confirmation of the Equivalence Principle, see Fox 2016 and Smith 2019.

Appendix B

Ontologies for Mechanics

A unit body is the basic entity out of which macroscopic bodies given to perception can be assembled via forces, charges, potentials, or some other type of physical agency. Matter theory, qua foundation for mechanics, distinguishes three kinds of unit body: the mass point, the rigid body, and the deformable continuum. Kant had custom names for them: physical monad, absolutely hard body, and infinitely divisible matter, respectively.[1] These fundamental kinds are mutually irreducible; none can be described (nor explained) in terms of the other two. They differ from one another in regard to size, mobility, and causal actions. I go over them in turn.

Size

What really determines body size is the way that *mass* is distributed over space. In a mass point, the entire mass is located at a Euclidean point, whose size is zero. Around that point there is a volume (usually spherical) filled by an acceleration field, *not* mass – so, it does not count toward body size. A rigid body is a finite volume with mass distributed at *every* point inside it. Finally, in a deformable continuum, the least part is an infinitesimal volume dV, with mass density having a positive value at every such volume element. Intuitively, if a macroscopic body is a physical continuum, it is filled everywhere with mass; and if it is an aggregate of mass points or of rigids, there is empty space inside the volume that counts as its proper volume.

Motion

Let a unit body move from place A to place B. If that body is a mass point, its trajectory is a skew curve, with A and B as its endpoints; in the degenerate case, that curve is a straight line. Three coordinates are enough to describe its position at any instant, and also its change in position over time, namely, its rate of motion. If it is a rigid body, its overall motion is a combination of a pure translation (whereby all its points have the same velocity) and a rigid rotation

---

[1] In the ontology of 'mathematico-mechanical investigators of nature,' rigid bodies were microscopic. For those entities, he used the term 'fundamental corpuscle' [*Grundkörperchen*]. Caveat: Kant in *Foundations* does have the term 'rigid' [*starr*]. But it is a misnomer; he does not use it in the modern sense above. By rigid, he means our current notion of 'stiff,' i.e., highly resistant to deformation, relative to a spectrum of applied force. We mean rigid in the sense of *impossible* to deform – ours is a modal notion. The eighteenth-century name for our concept was 'hard body.'

Appendix B

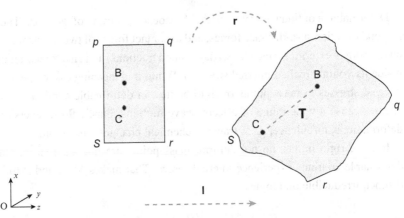

Figure 13 The general motion of deformable continua. Left: a continuous body *spqr* at some time *e*. Right: the same body at a later time *f*, after forces have acted on it. Its motion from *e* to *f* is a combination of three distinct kinds of displacement: a rigid translation l, a rigid rotation r, and a deformation T. By means of T, any two points B, C in the body can change their mutual distance; so, the whole body can stretch or compress in arbitrary directions.

(of the whole body) around its center of mass. Finally, a continuous body's motion is a combination of pure translation, rigid rotation, and deformation (whereby any two points B, C in the body change their relative distance; see Figure 13).

Note that these motions are conceptually tied to their sui generis unit-body. Specifically, a mass point neither rotates nor deforms – such motions are meaningless in regard to it. And a rigid body does not deform – that too is a meaningless motion for that type of object.

Actions

These species of unit body are radically distinct because of the type of force they can exert on another body of their kind.

Point masses interact only by action-at-a-distance forces: attraction, repulsion, or sideways acceleration. Contact between points is not a meaningful notion, so these bodies cannot exert mutual contact forces.

Rigid bodies induce two kinds of actions: forces at a distance and also contact forces. For the latter species, there is a caveat. These contact forces act just on the bounding surface of the body; they cause no actions within the body – which, qua rigid, cannot deform internally and must remain self-congruent at all times. So, contact actions on a rigid mass induce just whole-body translations, rigid rotations, or both.

Deformable continua engage in the broadest spectrum of actions. They respond to action-at-a-distance forces, and to contact forces of two kinds: forces on the body's exterior surface (nowadays called tractions) and also forces acting inside its volume (called internal stresses). While it is meaningless to speak of internal stresses in mass points or rigid bodies, in deformable continua these stresses cause a wide range of effects: wave motions, plastic flow, reversible deformations, turbulence, mass transfer, chemical changes, and so on.

In sum, rigid bodies do not deform, mass points are not finite-sized, and deformable continua experience internal forces. That makes M, P, and R fully distinct, irreducible ontologies.

Bibliography

I cite canonically from the Academy Edition: *Kant's Gesammelte Schriften*. G. Reimer/De Gruyter (1903–). *Foundations* and *Prolegomena* are in volume 4; *Monads* is in 1, and *Motion* in 2. Moreover, I rely on an excellent modern edition: Kant, I. 1997. *Metaphysische Anfangsgründe der Naturwissenschaft*, ed. K. Pollok. Felix Meiner.

Secondary Sources

Adickes, E. 1924. *Kant als Naturforscher*. De Gruyter.
Ameriks, K. 1978. Kant's transcendental deduction as a regressive argument. *Kant Studien* 69: 273–287.
Anstey, P. and J. Schuster (eds.). 2005. *The Science of Nature in the Seventeenth Century*. Springer.
Basile, G. P. 2013. *Kants Opus postumum und seine Rezeption*. De Gruyter.
Bennett, J. 1966. *Kant's Analytic*. Cambridge University Press.
Biener, Z. and C. Smeenk. 2012. Cotes' queries: Newton's empiricism and conceptions of matter. *Interpreting Newton*, ed. E. Schliesser and A. Janiak, 105–137. Cambridge University Press.
Brading, K. and M. Stan. 2023. *Philosophical Mechanics in the Age of Reason*. Oxford University Press.
Calinger, R. 1969. The Newtonian-Wolffian Controversy: 1740–1759. *Journal of the History of Ideas* 30: 319–330.
Caparrini, S. and C. Fraser. 2013. Mechanics in the Eighteenth Century. *The Oxford Handbook of the History of Physics*, ed. J. Z. Buchwald and R. Fox, 358–405. Oxford University Press.
Cramer, K. 1985. *Nicht-reine synthetische Urteile a priori*. Carl Winter Universitätsverlag.
Earman, J. 1989. *World Enough and Space-Time*. MIT Press.
Euler, L. 1752a. Découverte d'un nouveau principe de mécanique. *Mémoires de l'académie des sciences* 6: 185–217. Berlin.
   1752b. Recherches sur l'origine des forces. *Mémoires de l'académie des sciences* 6: 409–447. Berlin.
   1765. *Theoria motus corporum solidorum seu rigidorum*, vol. I. Rostock.
Fox, C. 2016. The Newtonian equivalence principle: How the relativity of acceleration led Newton to the equivalence of inertial and gravitational mass. *Philosophy of Science* 83: 1027–1038.
Friedman, M. 1992. *Kant and the Exact Sciences*. Harvard University Press.

2012. Quantity of matter in the *Metaphysical Foundations of Natural Science*. *The Southern Journal of Philosophy* 50: 482–503.

2013. *Kant's Construction of Nature*. Cambridge University Press.

Gaukroger, S. 1982. The metaphysics of impenetrability: Euler's conception of force. *British Journal for the History of Science* 15: 132–154.

Hartz, G. 2007. *Leibniz's Final System: Monads, Matter and Animals*. Routledge.

Henrich, D. 1989. Kant's notion of a deduction and the methodological background of the First Critique. *Kant's Transcendental Deductions: The Three 'Critiques' and the 'Opus Postumum,'* ed. E. Förster, 27–46. Stanford University Press.

Hermann, J. 1716. *Phoronomia*. Amsterdam.

Hogan, D. 2007. Wolff on order and space. *Wolff und die europäische Aufklärung*, eds. J. Stolzenberg and O.-P. Rudolph, 29–42. G. Olms.

2020. Kant and the character of mathematical inference. *Kant's Philosophy of Mathematics. Vol. I: The Critical Philosophy and its Roots*, ed. C. Posy and O. Rechter, 126–154. Cambridge University Press.

Holden, T. 2004. *The Architecture of Matter: Galileo to Kant*. Oxford University Press.

Howard, S. 2023. *Kant's Late Philosophy of Nature*. Cambridge University Press.

Kant, I. 1992. *Theoretical Philosophy, 1755-1770*, ed. and trans. D. Walford and R. Meerbote. Cambridge University Press.

Kant, I. 2004. *Metaphysical Foundations of Natural Science*, ed. and trans. M. Friedman. Cambridge University Press.

Kant, I. 2012. *Natural Science*, ed. E. Watkins. Cambridge University Press.

Lagrange, J. L. 1788. *Mechanique analitique*. Paris.

Leduc, C. 2018. La *Monadologia physica* de Kant et le concours sur les monades de l'Académie de Berlin. *Akten des XII. Internationalen Kant-Kongresses*, ed. V. Waibel, M. Ruffing, and D. Wagner, 893–900. De Gruyter.

Leduc, C. and D. Dumouchel (eds.) 2015. La philosophie à l'Académie de Berlin au XVIIIe siècle. Special issue of *Philosophiques* 42.

Leibniz, G. W. 1989. On body and force, against the Cartesians. *Philosophical Essays*, ed. R. Ariew and D. Garber, 250–256. Hackett.

McLear, C. 2018. Motion and the affection argument. *Synthese* 195: 4979–4995.

McNulty, M. B. 2014. Kant on chemistry and the application of mathematics in natural science. *Kantian Review* 19: 393–418.

Messina, J. 2015. Conceptual analysis and the essence of space: Kant's Metaphysical Exposition revisited. *Archiv für Geschichte der Philosophie* 97: 416–457.

2018. Kant's stance on the relationalist-substantivalist debate and its justification. *Journal of the History of Philosophy* 56: 697–726.

Miller, A. and E. Miller. 1994. Introduction and commentary. P. Plaass 1994, 1–165.

Newton, I. 1687. *Philosophiae naturalis principia mathematica*. London.

1999. *The Principia*, ed. I. B. Cohen, trans. A. Whitman. University of California Press.

2014. De gravitatione et aequipondio fluidorum. *Philosophical Writings*, ed. A. Janiak, revised edition, 26–58. Cambridge University Press.

Parsons, C. 2012. Remarks on pure natural science. *From Kant to Husserl*, 69–79. Harvard University Press.

Plaass, P. 1994. *Kant's Theory of Natural Science*, ed. A. Miller and M. Miller. Springer.

Pollok, K. 2006. Kant's critical concepts of motion. *Journal of the History of Philosophy* 44: 559–575.

Rynasiewicz, R. 1995. 'By their properties, causes and effects:' Newton's scholium on time, space, place and motion. *Studies in History and Philosophy of Science* 26: 133–153.

Shabel, L. 1998. Kant on the 'symbolic construction' of mathematical concepts. *Studies in History and Philosophy of Science* 29: 589–621.

2005. Apriority and application. *Oxford Handbook of Philosophy of Mathematics and Logic*, ed. S. Shapiro, 29–50. Oxford University Press.

Smith, G. E. 2014. Closing the loop. *Newton and Empiricism*, ed. Z. Biener and E. Schliesser, 262–352. Oxford University Press.

2019. Newton's numerator in 1685: A year of gestation. *Studies in History and Philosophy of Modern Physics* 68: 163–177.

forthcoming. Experiments in the *Principia*. *Oxford Handbook of Isaac Newton*, ed. C. Smeenk and E. Schliesser. Oxford University Press.

Smith, S. 2013. Kant's picture of monads in the *Physical Monadology*. *Studies in History and Philosophy of Science* 44: 102–111.

2013. Does Kant have a pre-Newtonian picture of force in the balance argument? An account of how the balance argument works. *Studies in History and Philosophy of Science* 44: 470–480.

Stan, M. 2009. Kant's early theory of motion. *The Leibniz Review* 19: 29–61.

2013. Kant's third law of mechanics. *Studies in History and Philosophy of Science* 44: 493–504.

2014. Unity for Kant's natural philosophy. *Philosophy of Science* 81: 423–443.

2015. Absolute space and the riddle of rotation. *Oxford Studies in Early Modern Philosophy* vol. 7, ed. D. Garber and D. Rutherford, 257–308. Clarendon Press.

2017. Metaphysical foundations of neoclassical mechanics. *Kant and the Laws of Nature*, ed. M. Massimi and A. Breitenbach, 214–234. Cambridge University Press.

2019. Absolute time: The limit of Kant's idealism. *Noûs* 53: 433–461.

2022. Phoronomy: Space, construction, and mathematizing motion. *Kant's Metaphysical Foundations of Natural Science: A Critical Guide*, ed. M. B. McNulty, 80–97. Cambridge University Press.

2023. Beyond Newton, Leibniz and Kant: Insufficient foundations, 1687–1786. *Between Leibniz, Newton, and Kant: Philosophy and Science in the Eighteenth Century*, ed. W. Lefèvre, 295–310. Springer.

in press. Mechanics from Galileo to Lagrange. *The History and Philosophy of Science, 1450 to 1750*, ed. M. Stan. Bloomsbury.

Strawson, P. F. 1966. *The Bounds of Sense: An Essay on Kant's Critique of Pure Reason*. Methuen.

Walker, R. 1971. The status of Kant's theory of matter. *Synthese* 23: 121–126.

Watkins, E. 2006. On the necessity and nature of simples: Leibniz, Wolff, Baumgarten, and the Pre-Critical Kant. *Oxford Studies in Early Modern Philosophy*, vol. 3, ed. S. Nadler and D. Garber, 261–314. Clarendon Press.

2019. *Kant on Laws*. Cambridge University Press.

Wolff, C. 1720. *Vernünfftige Gedancken von Gott, der Welt und der Seele des Menschen*. Halle.

Acknowledgments

My greatest debt of gratitude is to Cherie McGill, whose love, selfless support, and clear-eyed advice have sustained and guided me from the beginning. I have benefitted from invaluable comments by Desmond Hogan, Eric Watkins, Aaron Wells, and Bennett McNulty. Many ideas in this work come from long-standing conversations I've had with Michael Friedman, Sheldon Smith, Katherine Brading, and George E. Smith. I thank them all gratefully.

Cambridge Elements

The Philosophy of Immanuel Kant

Desmond Hogan
Princeton University

Desmond Hogan joined the philosophy department at Princeton in 2004. His interests include Kant, Leibniz and German rationalism, early modern philosophy, and questions about causation and freedom. Recent work includes 'Kant on the Foreknowledge of Contingent Truths', *Res Philosophica* 91(1) (2014); 'Kant's Theory of Divine and Secondary Causation', in Brandon Look (ed.) *Leibniz and Kant*, Oxford University Press (2021); 'Kant and the Character of Mathematical Inference', in Carl Posy and Ofra Rechter (eds.) *Kant's Philosophy of Mathematics Vol. I*, Cambridge University Press (2020).

Howard Williams
University of Cardiff

Howard Williams was appointed Honorary Distinguished Professor at the Department of Politics and International Relations, University of Cardiff in 2014. He is also Emeritus Professor in Political Theory at the Department of International Politics, Aberystwyth University, a member of the Coleg Cymraeg Cenedlaethol (Welsh-language national college) and a Fellow of the Learned Society of Wales. He is the author of *Marx* (1980); *Kant's Political Philosophy* (1983); *Concepts of Ideology* (1988); *Hegel, Heraclitus and Marx's Dialectic* (1989); *International Relations in Political Theory* (1992); *International Relations and the Limits of Political Theory* (1996); *Kant's Critique of Hobbes: Sovereignty and Cosmopolitanism* (2003); *Kant and the End of War* (2012) and is currently editor of the journal Kantian Review. He is writing a book on the Kantian legacy in political philosophy for a new series edited by Paul Guyer.

Allen Wood
Indiana University

Allen Wood is Ward W. and Priscilla B. Woods Professor Emeritus at Stanford University. He was a John S. Guggenheim Fellow at the Free University in Berlin, a National Endowment for the Humanities Fellow at the University of Bonn and Isaiah Berlin Visiting Professor at the University of Oxford. He is on the editorial board of eight philosophy journals, five book series and The Stanford Encyclopedia of Philosophy. Along with Paul Guyer, Professor Wood is co-editor of The Cambridge Edition of the Works of Immanuel Kant and translator of the Critique of Pure Reason. He is the author or editor of a number of other works, mainly on Kant, Hegel and Karl Marx. His most recently published books are *Fichte's Ethical Thought*, Oxford University Press (2016) and *Kant and Religion*, Cambridge University Press (2020). Wood is a member of the American Academy of Arts and Sciences.

About the Series

This Cambridge Elements series provides an extensive overview of Kant's philosophy and its impact upon philosophy and philosophers. Distinguished Kant specialists provide an up-to-date summary of the results of current research in their fields and give their own take on what they believe are the most significant debates influencing research, drawing original conclusions.

Cambridge Elements

The Philosophy of Immanuel Kant

Elements in the Series

Kant's Theory of Labour
Jordan Pascoe

Kant's Late Philosophy of Nature: The Opus postumum
Stephen Howard

Kant on Freedom
Owen Ware

Kant on Self-Control
Marijana Vujošević

Kant on Rational Sympathy
Benjamin Vilhauer

The Moral Foundation of Right
Paul Guyer

The Postulate of Public Right
Patrick Capps and Julian Rivers

Kant on the History and Development of Practical Reason
Olga Lenczewska

Kant's Ideas of Reason
Katharina T. Kraus

Kant on Marriage
Charlotte Sabourin

Kant and Teleology
Thomas Teufel

Kant's Natural Philosophy
Marius Stan

A full series listing is available at: www.cambridge.org/EPIK

Printed by Integrated Books International,
United States of America